'This amazing book serves as a window to so much. First, into Richard's own journey, with his feelings recorded so personally and with such depth. Secondly, into our calling to be human with each other; to reach out to those around us going through experiences they may never share. Thirdly, into emotions and longings in us that may well have lain undetected until now. If ever there is a book to open our eyes to the wonder of living every day to the full, this is it!'

The Revd John Ryeland,
Director of The Christian Healing Mission

'A raw and honest journey through a grief that changes, but never ends. This deeply personal account is both moving and hopeful.'

Bishop Nick Baines

'If I'm honest, this is the book I never wanted to read; my chest tightens and my breath hurts just thinking about grief and the pain it inflicts. Yet it's an honest, rich narrative of deep steadfast love and friendship. Richard reflects on Fiona, sharing, "her illness frustrated, restricted and pained her, but it never defined her", and following her death he reflects on a "small prophet" and "Ginny, the rescue dog" and the impact they have on his ongoing journey. Richard's faith stands firm throughout, reflecting that in the complexity of bereavement the confidence of faith is not lost but takes on the nuance of life. *Postcards from the Land of Grief* is a beautifully crafted and creative approach to considering the impact of memories; it offers hope for a different future, informed by the gift of wisdom and time.'

Kath Evans, Director of Nursing (Children),
Barts Health NHS Trust

'Richard's heartfelt retelling of how he cared for Fiona during her time with cancer, and how his life changed after her death, is something we can all learn from. These "postcards from the land of grief" pour out with emotion and love between a man and wife.

'This is not just a guidebook for how to cope after the death of a loved one, this is a story of life and a celebration of that.'

Chris Byland, radio and content producer and
broadcaster

'A postcard is about all you can read when your brain is knocked out by grief. That's why this book works so well, not just for people on this ghastly journey, but also for those who struggle to help them.'

Jennifer Rees Larcombe,
bereavement and trauma counsellor

'When someone dies, whether they be someone we love or someone loved by a friend or relative, it can often be hard to find words to express our feelings. In this beautiful and searingly honest series of reflections, Richard Littledale has crafted words which not only speak of his own feelings but which also feel as though they speak of ours too.'

Paula R. Gooder, writer and speaker

'Powerful and poignant . . . Richard Littledale cleverly juxtaposes the complexity of grief with the medium of the humble postcard, sending a very personal message to anyone who's had to navigate their way through the world of bereavement and loss.'

Sarah Major, presenter and producer,
BBC Radio Sheffield

'Richard's writing is poignant, evocative and comforting all at once. I am confident this book will serve as a guiding light with which others can begin to navigate their own grief as they recognize their experiences and emotions within his honest narrative.'

Heidi Travis, Sue Ryder Chief Executive

Postcards from the Land of Grief

Comfort for the journey through loss towards hope

Richard Littledale

Authentic

First published 2019 by Authentic Media Limited,
PO Box 6326, Bletchley, Milton Keynes, MK1 9GG.
authenticmedia.co.uk

British Library Cataloguing in Publication Data
A catalogue record for this book is available from the British Library.
ISBN: 978-1-78893-071-0
978-1-78893-072-7 (e-book)

Royalties from the sale of this book will go to Sue Ryder: Sue Ryder is a charity
registered in England and Wales (1052076) and in Scotland (SC039578).
Company limited by guarantee registered in England and Wales (943228).
Registered office: Kings House, King Street, Sudbury, Suffolk CO10 2ED.

Cover and internal designs by Vivian Hansen
Printed and bound by CPI Group (UK) Ltd., Croydon, CR0 4YY

To every Sue Ryder nurse everywhere
— doing their best when life is the worst

Contents

Contents

Contents

Fiona Jane Littledale

A tribute delivered at her thanksgiving service, 16 November 2017

Consider this awkward moment if you will. You are driving home from Cornwall and there is nobody in the car except for you and your terminally ill wife. The conversation turns to what must be, to the thanksgiving service which also must be; and to what will be said. 'What one word would you use to describe me?' she asks . . .

I thought back over our thirty years of marriage, the birth and raising of our three magnificent sons. I thought back over four ministries with good times and bad. I thought back over seven years of cancer – with repeated rounds of chemo, surgeries and knock-backs of every kind. I thought back over her dedicated years of work in healthcare information. I remembered her support for her friends (which she would keep up until she was no longer able to hold a phone and text them), and I said . . . 'Steadfast' and waited for the reaction. That beloved smile, about which so many have written, spread across her lips, and she said, 'That's the nicest thing anyone ever said about me.'

Fiona was proud to wear that label of 'steadfast' – as wife, mother, colleague . . . and above all, as a woman of faith.

It is very rare at a thanksgiving for the person at the heart of it all to speak. However, on this occasion it is possible. Earlier this year I was teaching a course on the Disciple's Way, with each week illustrated through personal story. On the week where we talked about dying and journey's end, Fiona was supposed to share her story. It turned out to be the week when she received her terminal diagnosis, and so it was just not possible. Instead, I pass her own words on to you now:

In the shadows, ordinary objects can look much bigger and scarier than they really are. But I once heard someone describe how the shepherd would bang on the rocky valley sides to guide the sheep, and we have been aware throughout that we are not on our own in this distorted landscape.

We have been conscious of God's presence guiding and sustaining us, and of the prayers and love of his people. In the shadows, it is also easy to lose things and I have lost many things over the last few years. Tangible things like my hair, various internal organs and the feeling in my feet, and less tangible ones such as the expectation of a normal lifespan and all that would accompany that. But I have gained an appreciation for the here and now, and as an inveterate forward planner, the ability to live and enjoy a life segmented by scans into twelve-week blocks. The Danish think they invented the concept of *hygge*, hunkering down and enjoying the simple things, but actually we did.

Finally, the valley floor is often strewn with rocks. If you have ever been to Skrinkle Haven on the Pembrokeshire coast you will know that you drop down steeply from the coast path and literally scramble over the rocks on the valley floor before emerging onto the most beautiful beach. A beach really is my happy place, and I think I will have to scramble over some pretty big rocks in my next chapter, but when I emerge on the other side I will be more fully alive than ever before.

How true that proved to be . . . and how big the rocks were to be as well. She was steadfast – in love, in service and in faith. That trait was not shown in any severe way, though. Her steadfast resolve was tempered by a rich sense of humour and a deep appreciation of the value of friendship. Among the hundreds of letters and cards was one from an 11-year-old boy, written in his own hand, which described her as 'smiley', thanked her for always making time to talk to him, and said that he was very sorry she had died. His little sister talked of her 'chuckly laugh' – and many others have said similar things.

'Incarnation' means that God was made real in Christ. 'Incarnation' means that he is seen again in oh so human clothing, and wonderfully so. Like Paul in 2 Timothy 4:7, Fiona can now say: 'I have fought the good fight, I have finished the race, I have kept the faith.'

We will remember her in so many ways. Our backs will stand a little straighter when the trials come. Our hearts will stretch a little wider when a friend needs us and we give no thought to our own plans or timing. Our faith will run a little deeper when the cold wind blows. And by the grace of God, we shall all be a little more steadfast because of her. May God make it so . . . AMEN.

Richard Littledale

Part One

Entering the Land of Grief

1

The Chapter I Wanted to Write

What did you dream of doing when you grew up, I wonder? To be honest, I can't really remember what I dreamt of. I had a great-uncle who had driven a steam train – and so that probably featured at some point. I would guess that watching the Apollo space missions probably sowed one or two astronaut ambitions in my head too. The odd school play made me dream of acting on the stage, and later studies in English Literature made me think about directing behind it.

Whatever these dreams might have been, the idea that I might serve as an ordained minister, let alone write a book on my experiences as one, would have been out of the question. Church was not part of my experience in early childhood, and but for the Gideons I would never have visited one. When they came to my secondary school in the hot summer of 1976, they issued a New Testament to every first-year student, with the only requirement being that we should try to read it. I still have it now, the date of its issue written in my schoolboy handwriting, and smudged by an accidental leak from my sports bottle.

Straight away, I dipped into some of the pages labelled 'Where to find Help when', and found that they were indeed helpful. Beyond that, though, I had very little idea how to use this strange book. A teacher suggested at our next assembly that those who were struggling with this unfamiliar book might find some help at the Christian Union, which he ran in one of the science labs at lunchtime. Curious to know more, I started to attend.

As time went by, that same teacher told those attending the Christian Union that he ran another club at weekends. It was called 'Crusaders' and met in the local Baptist church on Sunday afternoons, with occasional extra activities on Saturdays. I started to attend and soon made friends, as well as getting to grips more with the Bible. Out of curiosity, I attended a service of believer's baptism at the church. Whilst much of what took place was unfamiliar, I was impressed immediately with the sincerity of those who were declaring their faith in this way. I continued to attend and found that the same sincerity was there every week – in the welcomers on the door, the preachers at the front and the leaders of the church's youth group. Over time, I would come to understand the deep and genuine Christian faith which made them all behave this way – and I would embrace it for myself. At the age of 16, I underwent believer's baptism and looked to see where God would lead me next.

Two years later, I left home to study at the University of St Andrews. Like every other Scottish university at the time, my offer of a place to study was from my chosen Faculty, rather than any particular subject. Consequently, I began my university career studying French, German and Arabic. My relationship with the latter would prove to be short-lived. Overwhelmed by the new alphabet, and not at all sure that it was for me, I exchanged Arabic for Theology, and thus began a path which would affect the rest of my life. I would go on to read Biblical Studies alongside the foreign languages in my second year, and would opt for a combined degree in French and Practical Theology.

After my third year of study, I took a year out to use my French in the context of church-based mission in Belgium. The experience refined my understanding of what church and mission were all about – and made me appreciate the nuanced challenges of communicating across cultures and languages. There were lessons I learned when crossing a linguistic gap in my stumbling French which I would later employ when crossing other gaps in English. So often, the first part of speaking is listening. It was also in Belgium that I started learning to preach – an interesting challenge in a foreign language. To this day, I still preach from very longhand notes – a

5

habit which I formed when every word had to be carefully chosen and remembered!

Back home from Belgium, and now engaged to be married, it was time to think about the future. Maybe it was inevitable that my combined studies should affect my choice of career. The young man who had entered university wanting to train as a theatre director no longer found the idea so appealing. Perhaps I should pursue an avenue which would make more direct use of my studies and provide a more obvious outlet for my growing appetite for theology? The trouble is, I had always believed that it was a mistake when people went directly from university into training for ordained ministry without an intervening period in the workplace. I bided my time and waited for the obvious workplace door to swing open. It did not. By the time I was in my last year at St Andrews, my sense of conviction about ministry was growing stronger by the day. Convinced that I should demonstrate my willingness to embrace this surprising calling, I cancelled all my applications for other jobs and applied to train for Baptist ministry.

At this point in my life I had the most wonderful woman, Fiona, by my side. Our relationship had started shortly before I left for Belgium – and had stood the tests which distance imposed upon it. Now both in the same country again, we knew that our paths belonged together, but had no certainty about where they would lead. We had a date to get married, but no job or home to go to. God would provide.

I think it would be fair to say that pursuing a lifetime's calling by payphone from Scotland proved to be something of a challenge. If I thought that my hurried phone call, with the wind off the North Sea rattling the phone box windows, would sort out the future direction of my life, I was wrong. After numerous trips down south and a searching interview or two, I finally secured a place as a 'ministerial apprentice' at Hertford Baptist Church. Fiona and I got married in Fife, took our honeymoon on the island of Islay, and then moved all our worldly goods into a terraced cottage in our trusty VW Beetle. This was where the calling to ministry would be proved . . . or broken.

It turned out that I took to some aspects of it like a duck to water. Although it demanded a lot of preparation, preaching felt like the most natural thing in the world to me – and people listening appeared to feel the same. Behind the scenes, though, in pastoral situations, it was a different matter. I found the whole business of 'stepping into' other people's lives desperately hard. So many of their experiences were outside my own. Some were facing redundancy, others marital conflict or depression, and others were coming to terms with chronic illness. For me, the hardest of all was to provide care and help to those who were facing their own mortality. What on earth did this inexperienced young man have to say to those who were contemplating the end of their own life or that of a person they loved?

Sitting at the bedside of a dear, elderly Christian who was approaching her end, I felt anything but confident. I was unsure about what to say or how to say it. In the end I did the only thing I could think of – I sang, all alone, the old hymns which I thought she would know, and so the time passed. On other occasions I would read out words of Scripture, unsure whether the person in the bed could hear them. I would hold their hand, taking care not to disturb cannulas carrying vital fluids into their bodies, and I would try to pray. In truth, I felt unable to do the right thing, and unsure of my abilities.

By this point I was studying once again – part-time alongside my duties as a minister. When the opportunity came to research a dissertation, I knew just what I wanted to do. Somehow, I wanted to understand that hardest pastoral encounter better. Could I learn some-thing from my 'strong' moments in the pulpit which I could carry into the weak ones at the bedside? Then again, maybe the traffic could go back the other way? If I understood what was going on in those moments when I felt my weakness so acutely, perhaps they could help me in the strong ones too.

Christ in the dying

The first thing I discovered was something which most undergraduates find when they study some new and radical topic – that it is not so new and radical after all. Intellectuals and practitioners had been there long before me, of course. As I started to study, I listened in on the nuns in Mother Teresa's 'Home for dying incur-ables' in Kolkata. Each morning the nuns would start their day with the following prayer:

> Dearest Lord, may I see you today and every day in the person of your sick, and whilst serving them, minister unto you.

They weren't the only ones. In the Republic of Ireland, nursing order the Sisters of Charity would replace the name over the beds of those patients closest to death with the name 'Jesus'. Taking the words of Jesus in Matthew 25 to heart, they were saying that Jesus was *actually there* in the weak and the dying – those very people who had made me feel so inept as a pastor.

Pursuing the studies further, I found plenty of theologians willing to say that God could be seen more in moments of weakness than in strength. Jesus on the cross may tell us more about the character of God than Jesus striding confidently across the water or passing out bread and fish to the 5,000. Broken humanity, like a broken mirror might reflect the face of God in thousands of brilliant shards rather than one single image.

Christ in the carer

If this were so, then caring for the dying was a place not so much of fear, but revelation. A pastor caring for someone near their end – even an inept and junior pastor – might expect to meet God in such a place. In fact, he might expect not just to meet him there – but to *bring* him there. Trusting in a broken Saviour, and believing that God embraces humanity in the hardest moments – this might not be something to shrink from nearly so much as I had imagined.

On something of a roll, I began to see this in all sorts of places. I saw people in the Old Testament trailing across the desert after Moses, learning things they could never have learned if they stayed at home. I saw King David learning more about God as he toppled from his throne than ever he did whilst occupying it. I saw people like Paul and Peter meeting God in prison in a way they could never have done whilst free. I heard the prophet Isaiah talking about 'treasures of darkness' (Isaiah 45:3, ESV) which could only be found in the hardest time – without ever knowing how dear that verse would become to me one day.

The dent in ministry

If all these things were true, then maybe my encounters with people in the hardest moments might not so much challenge my ministry as dent it. Just as the patina on an antique brings age and colour to it, so the scratched and dented surface of theological certainty might better reflect the face of God. The more I researched this dissertation, the more convinced I became that those encounters with the dying from which I recoiled could really teach me something. Not only that, but the lessons I was learning at the bedside could equip me in so many other settings. They might make me preach different sermons, proffer different advice and hold different conversations.

The sermons would be different, because they would recognize the fragility of the life lived by many of those who heard them. It is not that they would lose their confidence, but rather that the confidence would find a different voice. It would be a voice more woodwind than brass – a note *formed* from the instrument like the instrument itself had been formed from the wood and the tree. Years later, I would read *The Jazz of Preaching* by Kirk Byron Jones. He would compare preaching to blues music, which emerged from great suffering, and say:

> When it comes to preaching through times of emotional strain and pain, the question is not how to preach when your heart is not in it. The question is how to preach with a different heart, a wounded heart.[1]

How right he would prove to be, and how little I knew then. The times would come, especially at Easter, when I would find myself preaching from just such a wounded heart.

Conversations and advice would be different too. It is not that they would lose the confidence of faith – but that they would gain the nuance of life. An ear tuned to hear God in the weakened voice of the dying might listen for him more intently in other conversations too. Maybe I would be like the hospice chaplain whom I met whilst writing the dissertation. He worked in a major London hospice, where many of the patients stayed for ten days or less before dying. Asked about the impact on his faith he paused, then replied with a twinkle in his eye:

Since working here, I know less,
but I believe more.

This was new territory for me. It was like stepping out of a forest of tall trees whose name was certainty. They occasionally blocked out the sun – but their trunks were straight as a die and they protected you from the heat of the sun. Stepping out into unbroken sunlight made me blink and shade my eyes. Gradually, though, they adjusted to the glare. Beyond the forest was an undulating landscape of hills and valleys – light and shade. The forest had been nice, but this was undoubtedly a more interesting landscape. Faith would wear different clothes here, I sensed – but it might also thrive and grow in a way it had never done before.

Maybe it would prove to be like the desert into which Moses led the people of Israel. It was a harsh and unforgiving place – where the comforts he once knew in the royal palace would be scarcely more than a distant memory. It would also be the place where he understood as never before that God goes behind and before his own – and provides both safe passage and provisions for those who require them.

Maybe it would be like the cleft in the rock to which the prophet Elijah fled after his bruising encounter with the prophets of Baal on Mount Carmel. This was a lonely and isolated place, where Elijah would encounter the depths of his exhaustion and the cost of his calling as never before. It was also a place where he learned that God provides even for the weary and dejected spokesman.

Maybe it would be like the wilderness, into which Christ was driven by the Holy Spirit after his baptism. This would be a place of hunger, attack and acute challenge for him – the voice of the devil loud in Christ's loneliness and weakness. It would also be the place where his calling would be voiced and defended as never before.

Maybe it would be like Patmos – an island penal colony to which the apostle John was sent as punishment for his loyalty to Christ. Here he was kept from the fellowship of his beloved church on the mainland and subjected to the harshest of treatment. Here too, though, he would encounter the risen Christ with such searing clarity that his vision still makes us blink twenty centuries later.

Wherever I was heading in this new territory, I sensed that it held the scope for both blessing and challenge, hope and fear. It turns out that I would discover most of its depths many years later.

The next chapter

The dissertation was an undergraduate one, stretching to not much more than forty pages. To be honest, I had done little more than crack open the lid of this

Pandora's box and peek at what was inside. I had asked some questions which had never occurred to me before. I had exposed some gaps of which I had been unaware. There was scope to take this further. However, with the demands of ordained ministry snapping at my heels, I quietly closed it and moved on. I would have loved to have studied this more. This place, where a mutable and passible God could be encountered in a moment of human suffering, was one in which I had not been before. The questions it asked, and the light it cast on my erstwhile certainties threw many things into sharp relief. However, the time was not right. For now, I would live with what I knew and put those questions aside.

When I read it now, there is a kind of irritating naivety to the words I wrote. Maybe we all feel that about words which we wrote a long time ago. Take these, for example:

> As their illness passes beyond the point where the doctors can check its progress, it is increasingly to the spiritual carer that they will turn with the dreadful impotency of their lives.

Twenty-five years later, I would find myself living that particular sentence within the confines of my own home, with theological study the thing furthest from my mind.

2

The Chapter I Didn't
Want to Write

By the time this chapter began my wife, Fiona, and I had been married for twenty-two years. God had given us three wonderful sons, and we had served in three different churches. Our first church was in Hertford, the county town of Hertfordshire. I was the first ministerial assistant to serve there, and the church had numerous families who were long established in the town. After five years in Hertford we moved to Purley, just near Croydon. At the time, the church was one of the biggest Baptist churches in the country, with more than 450 members. I served as part of a team of three, and learned so much from the gentle wisdom and wit of my senior minister. After five years in Purley, 1997 saw us move to Teddington, to the west of London.

Teddington would prove to be my longest ministry to date. During my nineteen years there, I saw the church staff team expand, the buildings redeveloped, and a new and exciting relationship forged with the local community. The latter involved both businesses and schools in all sorts of different initiatives. It was whilst working with the schools on a Christmas outreach project that this story began. We had invited local schools to bring their children on a 'Christmas journey' through a series of tents set up inside the church. The first was a 'story tent' where I told the story of creation to each new group of children, and set up the prospect of some-one coming to put it all right. The next tent was Mary's kitchen, where she was busy baking bread when the angel Gabriel visited her with the news of Jesus' birth. After that, the children progressed to the stable tent, where puppets of a cow and a sheep took up the story. The next tent, smelling of exotic spices, was crammed with gifts so that the children could fill a bag with gifts they thought the baby Jesus might like. Finally, they as-sembled in a tent set up as a modern living room, com-plete with hearth. Here, the story was brought right up to date before they left.

At the precise moment this chapter began, I was kneel-ing on the floor of the stable tent, propping up a back-drop behind the manger with my elbow as the puppets of a cow and a sheep had a conversation about the birth of Jesus. Earlier that morning, I had left Fiona at home, as she was not working that day. She had been troubled by acute stomach pains on and off for a little while, but met them with her customary courage and deter-mination. On that particular day, I didn't even know that a phone call had been made to the doctor whilst I was working with the children. Whilst I was ushering children through the church, she had made her way, painfully, to the doctor's surgery. Unknown to me, he

19

was astonished that she had made the trip on foot, and promptly said that she should be sent to the local hospital. The first I knew was when the screen of my mobile lit up and displayed the words 'in back of ambulance, talk later, F x'. This was to be the start of a long and costly journey.

That hospital visit extended for several days, with Fiona coming out just in time for Christmas. When the New Year came around, there were further tests. I remember clearly being summoned to Fiona's bedside so that the oncologist could pass on the news. Years later, we would reflect that if ever tea were offered, the news was probably bad. If tea and biscuits were offered, it was very grave. On this particular occasion, tea and biscuits were offered, and the consultant perched awkwardly on the edge of the bed, struggling to find the right words. These latest tests had revealed the presence of a significantly sized bowel tumour which had to be removed.

A gruelling course of chemotherapy began, followed by surgery and then more chemotherapy. The next twelve months were swallowed up in a miasma of treatments, check-ups, hospital visits and consultations. Throughout the chemotherapy, our lives became inextricably linked to the cycle of medication, recovery, waiting and starting again. It was a measure of how much our lives had changed when we got excited about a high white cell blood count (meaning that treatment could proceed) or deflated by a low one (meaning that it could not, and the whole process would take longer). In the end, the last dose of chemotherapy was delivered on New Year's Eve 2010. We drove home through the darkness, Fiona dozing fitfully, and hoped for better things. Check-ups stretched out over the months, the gap gradually widening from three to six months as we went. The relief when it was all over was palpable . . . and short-lived.

The cancer was set to return in both lungs, the adrenal gland, and finally in the abdomen. During the respite months we made the most of the strength Fiona had – cherishing every moment with our wonderful boys and travelling three times to different parts of Italy. Our first trip was to Sorrento, in the south of that country. As I write now, I can hear the sound of Fiona's laugh as I told her that the hat she wore in the blistering streets of Pompeii made her look like a Victorian missionary. The second trip was very different – further north around the elegant shores of Lake Garda. The water had its usual captivating effect on both of us, and we had many walks, holding hands, along the shore of the lake as the sun set over the horizon. Our last trip was to Venice.

We loved the colours and reflections, and savoured more than once the cool shade of a tree-lined square in the Jewish Quarter. It is only when I look back now that I realize the walks we took on those holidays were getting shorter and shorter. The cancer was exacting its toll, out of sight but very definitely not out of mind.

On all our holidays, it became something of a habit to take photographs looking out from a café or restaurant at the view. There were certain rules which applied: neither of us featured in the picture, there had to be a corner of the table in the picture, and wherever possible a bit of window or awning to frame the view. In this way, looking at the picture made you feel as if you were back there eating or drinking again. I have a whole collection of these photos taken from places as far apart as Picardy in northern France and Ravello in southern Italy. To be honest, I am quite tempted to look at them now whenever I eat alone.

In late 2015, there was a brief lull in the cancer's onslaught. If we were to move on and tackle a new church together, then it was now or never. A church we had looked at early in that year, before the latest episode, was still advertising, and so we began a conversation. A phone call with the head of the search team confirmed that I might indeed be the kind of minister they were looking for. An initial visit to the church together for me to preach was followed by a meeting with the search team, a meeting with the deacons and further reflection by both parties. The first Saturday of 2016 saw Fiona and I meeting with the deacons of the church for a whole morning and talking things through. In the February of that year, we travelled to Newbury again for various meetings on the Saturday, followed by a 'preach with a view' on the Sunday. When Fiona and I stopped at a country pub on our way home for lunch, I reached across the table and held her hand as I wished her 'Happy Valentine's Day'. It had been an unusual way to spend it. Throughout the process, Fiona brought her wisdom, discernment and steadfast faith to bear. When we made the decision to move, and went through the delicate business of telling a church where we had invested nineteen years of our lives that it was time to go, her steadying hand kept me upright again and again.

In the summer of 2016, after nineteen years in Teddington, we moved to Newbury in Berkshire. We both began to make all the adjustments necessary to setting up a new life. There is nothing like moving house to make you question the value of all your accumulated clutter, and I'm sure I reached the point where the car could drive to the recycling centre all by itself! We became very familiar with the local home stores too, where Fiona's keen eye soon picked out the right curtains for the right windows. We enjoyed setting up a new home together, and found lots of lovely places to visit in the surrounding Berkshire countryside.

Of course, the home was only half of it. There was a new church to meet too. Over the first few months, I invested time in leaders and deacons, and Fiona was keen to open our new home for an early social with the deacons and their families. At church, whilst I was mainly up at the front, she was in amongst the congregation – making friends with old and young alike. She was always keen to hear their stories – whether of new schools and children or the problems of old age. On one occasion she told me with a sparkle in her eye about how she and one of the church's oldest members had joked that perhaps they should take up Zumba together! People loved her, and she loved them back. There was so much promise to this new chapter of our lives. There were clouds just over the horizon, though.

One of the difficulties about moving house when you have a chronic condition like cancer is that you have to move hospitals and specialists too. It was a real wrench for Fiona to leave the oncologist at Kingston Hospital who had guided her with such wisdom, honesty and care through the years of treatment there. Instead, a whole new relationship had to be forged with a new specialist at the Churchill Hospital, in Oxford. We soon fell into a rhythm of visits there, gradually getting to know the oncology team. Like the ones we had left behind in Kingston, they were compassionate, wise and immensely skilled. The cancer had not gone, and this was confirmed just a few months after moving. Each new visit to the hospital made it clearer that it was still active and aggressive. Finally, on Maundy Thursday of 2017, a gentle and compassionate oncology professor told us that nothing more could be done. He was very honest, and discussed with us the infinitesimally small difference that treatment would make to life expectancy at that stage. It would change little, but would cost much in terms of symptoms in whatever time was left. Instead, he handed Fiona's care over to the local palliative care team, and we would make no more visits to the hospital.

We squeezed a lot into the months which followed. As the cancer got worse it felt a bit like trying to outrun a gathering storm. The trouble was that, as the storm got closer, Fiona got weaker and slower – so it was sure to catch up with her sooner or later. We gathered many of the family together in a cottage in Pembrokeshire, and savoured the views of the rugged coast which we loved so much. Together, the two of us travelled to Cornwall – a place which neither of us really knew. Although our walks were necessarily short ones, we made the most of them. I often come across a photo now, taken in the churchyard of the church of St Just in the Roseland Peninsula. The church is a hidden gem, tucked away in lush gardens on a bend in the river estuary. In the photo, Fiona is looking away from the camera as she looks up at the church. Photographs are deceptive things, as they freeze forever a moment which cannot come again. If I were to visit that churchyard again, I almost feel as if I would go looking for her – wearing her purple coat and just about to walk inside. Back home, we savoured little trips out and often sat by sparkling water together, thinking and talking.

By the early autumn, our house became the epicentre of a whirl of medical care. There were palliative care nurses, practice nurses, GPs, stair lift engineers, oxygen nurses, occupational therapists and others all visiting the house. If I look back at my diary now, I see a tapestry of medical appointments stretching throughout that time. The house itself changed so much, so quickly. A stair lift appeared on the stairs, a disability stool in the shower, a handle on the side of the bed to get in and out; and an oxygen machine – whirring and hissing in the corner. All these things were designed to make life easier, but they also had the effect of making our home feel less and less like our home. I suspect that I was more aware of that than Fiona. For her, they were simply the means of making life sustainable without leaving our home and my side.

As October wore on, Fiona was in more and more pain as the cancer continued its voracious march through her cells. If we went out at all it was for increasingly short trips, and never without the wheelchair. We soon discovered that places which described themselves as 'wheelchair friendly' were not that friendly at all. Rutted gravel paths were impassable, and a short cut across the grass could prove to be a dead end. On one occasion we got caught unawares by a grating in the roadside just behind a parking space. On that day, I came very close to pitching Fiona out of the chair and headlong into the road. Nobody tells you these things when you start to use a wheelchair. As the month continued, that became less and less of an issue. Fiona rarely left the house, and saw little apart from the view from sofa or bed.

Unbelievably loyal to the last – she was still texting friends in need and encouraging them right up until the time when she could no longer hold a phone. Her illness frustrated, restricted and pained her, but it never defined her.

November 6th was a beautiful morning, with winter sunshine catching all the sparkly frost on the plants. At Fiona's suggestion, I went out early with my camera to catch the beauty. I went to Greenham Common, just up the road, and set eyes for the first time on The Courage Tree, about which I shall write more further on. Later on, we decided that a short trip out together would be good, so we made some sandwiches and decided to head for Dorchester Abbey near Oxford. Together we visited the abbey, gazing up at its soaring height and enjoying its history. I sensed that Fiona needed some time to pray, and for a little while she paused in the wheelchair gazing up at the East Window.

Once we had seen all that the abbey had to offer, we headed outside to find somewhere to eat our lunch. Over the years, unsuitable picnics had become something of a forte of ours. On one occasion during a holiday in France, we crossed the border into Switzerland, only to be beaten back by the driving rain. We ate our picnic in a lay-by, wiping the steam off the windows every few minutes to remind us that Switzerland was still out there. On our first holiday in Italy, Fiona and I had stumbled upon tins of ready-made tuna salad in the supermarket. Together with some crackers as a spoon, we found that these made for a convenient picnic. Unfortunately, they had a down side. When we sat in Sorrento harbour watching the rich and elegant people stepping off the ferry from the island of Capri, the smell of our tuna salads brought every stray cat in Sorrento out to greet us. We never did that again!

The only place which the abbey had to eat our lunch was a solitary bench overlooking a woodland glade behind the church. Crossing the grass to get to it was something of a challenge, as the grass was soft and the wheelchair kept sinking into it. In the end, I had to turn it round and go backwards. This completed, we sat down with our little lunch – two best friends sharing a bite and a chat. It was really too cold to sit, and Fiona had little appetite, so we finished up and repeated the cumbersome journey across the grass. We negotiated the narrow pavements back to the car, Fiona slid into her seat with some difficulty, and I packed up the wheelchair and slotted it into the boot. As it turned out, this was to be our last-ever trip out together.

From late that afternoon began a downward spiral which no one could stop. Medical teams came and went over the hours which followed, but each new shot of pain relief had less effect than the last. Evening turned into night – and still they kept coming. The family began to make their way home from near and far by plane, train and car as night turned to day. Shortly before 9.30 a.m. Fiona, who was struggling by then to move at all, sat straight up. A few minutes later, the bravest woman I have ever met took one last breath and died in my arms. This was to be a day quite unlike the previous one. No frost and sparkle now but rain streaking down the windows – as if the world were mourning.

Part Two

Postcards from the Land of Grief

3

Why the Postcards?

I have always loved to write. Where other parents had to find room on their fridges or pinboards for their children's pictures, I suspect that mine did the same with stories. For that, I feel, they must share some of the blame. I grew up in a home where every available wall space was covered with bookshelves and we were always encouraged to take down any book we fancied and have a look. Friends coming round would comment on the number of books, although to me it was normal. I had a voracious appetite for books, and worked my way through my parents' childhood favourites, before finding others of my own.

Not surprisingly, this appetite for reading gave rise to an appetite for writing too. Stories were my favourite – giving vent to a vivid childhood imagination. After that came poetry, and then other types of writing as I went on through school. That particular journey continued – through three degrees in two different institutions. On both occasions where I was given the option, I substituted an examined course for an extended dissertation. In short: I really loved to write.

My early years in ministry would see me write a short guidebook on church communications for the Baptist Union, and occasional articles for Christian journals.

I also went on to contribute to a dictionary on biblical imagery and to write introductions to the four Gospels for a Bible handbook. When a publisher was handed one of my narrative sermons in 2001 and loved it, it was to be the start of something. They said that if I would like to write something, they would like to publish it – and so a partnership was born. It would lead to three titles with them on preaching and storytelling.

In 2011, I wrote a little Christmas story for a children's event at the church where I was working. More in hope than expectation, I put out a plea to get it published in time for Christmas, in aid of a local children's hospice. In a remarkable feat of international collaboration, it was illustrated, formatted, printed and put on sale within twenty-nine days. A couple of years later it was 'discovered' by a publisher, and is now on sale in English and French language versions. Other children's stories have followed. The little boy who was writing stories was now writing them for other boys and girls . . . and loving it.

Given all that I have written above, you might think that I would take to writing postcards like a duck to water. You would be wrong. Many times, the prospect of writing postcards has made me resentful and irritable on holiday. I could never think what to write, and they always felt like an unwelcome intrusion into time which was supposed to be leisure. Under sufferance, I would write them in the first day or two of a holiday, so as to be rid of the task. Into the postbox they would go – often covered in large writing for economy of words. Even the words which were there were largely predictable and unimaginative. They usually covered the journey from home, the weather, and maybe a brief description of other things that were planned. They read like the words of someone who had to write, rather than someone who wanted to.

So why, when I found myself in the harsh landscape of grief on that sad winter's day, did I start to write them again? It was not a deliberate thing. In the numbness of my initial shock at losing Fiona I was not really sure what I would write nor where I would write it. We had talked during the last weeks of her life about my writing, and I confessed that I thought a broken heart might be unequal to the task. I thought that the colossal shock of losing her might close my writing down for good. She was unconvinced, and said as she was propped up on the pillows that I could always write about 'this'.

Ever since the autumn of 2009, my blog had been the place for most of my writing output. It was a space for writing which was less 'finished' than a book, or even a journal article. It was a place where I could raise questions without the obligation to answer them. I saw the blog as a means whereby conversations could be begun with the reader – which might be continued . . . or might not. There was no need for a post to be overly finished, or polished, because I could always continue the conversation another day. If I were to write at all in the midst of this particular storm, it would surely be there.

One week after Fiona died, I took an early morning walk to the green cemetery where my father's remains are buried – and where hers would eventually rest. The family were sleeping at home, the funeral was still two days away, and I was in the mood for a long and undisturbed walk. The day was bitterly cold, as it had been the previous week, and I could see my breath as I crunched across the frosty grass. I took a photo of my shadow across the frost-dusted grass, and reflected how long it looked. Come to that, it struck me that everything looked different, even in a familiar place.

At that moment, the first postcard which you will read in the next chapter was born.

In some ways the postcard format seemed natural because I felt as if I were away from home. At times the pain of grief felt like a gnawing homesickness for the place where I used to live, and I missed it so much. Writing a 'postcard' on the blog was like writing to someone who lived in that old familiar place to which I could not return. That was the case whether I was writing the postcards in a notebook stood in a cemetery, on a tablet in an airport, or a laptop at my desk. The emotional ground beneath my feet had shifted so much that nothing was as it had been. There was no familiar ground, even in familiar places. It was like living abroad — even when walking down familiar streets and seeing familiar faces. Home was a long way away, and it felt as if I ought to drop someone a postcard to let them know I was OK.

There was something pleasantly unfinished about the postcard as a medium too. Postcards are not meant to be long, drawn-out explanations. Instead, they are snapshots – incomplete word pictures of the place where the writer finds him or herself. They can be not so much 'wish you were here' as 'I am here and this is what I see'. The limited space which they offer, and their context on the back of a photograph means that they are a brief explanation at best. They give a flavour of where the writer is to be found – no more. Fuller explanations must be delivered in person, and at a later date. A post-card is not a travelogue, written long after the journey is over from the comforts of home. A postcard is a verbal snapshot, no more.

In keeping with the nature of the postcard, I never had a specific plan to write the ones which you read in sub-sequent pages. When something struck me about this peculiar landscape of grief – whether how it looked or how it made me feel – I wrote it down. Sometimes I would write every day for three or four days. On other occasions, it might be weeks between the postcards. In a sense, I allowed the landscape rather than anything else to dictate their frequency. There were certain mile-stones along that journey during my first year of grief where I knew I would write them – a bit like knowing that you will write home from the top of the mountain, or the bottom of the world if you can. These included my 100th day as a widower (*Day 100*), Fiona's birthday

(*Nothing Planned*), and my wedding anniversary (*Distant Figures*). Somehow, I always had the feeling that I would write my last postcard on the anniversary of her death. To date, *The Last Postcard?* has been just that, but who knows?

A New Topography

I am learning that the landscape of grief is a strangely unnerving place. In part its strangeness is that those things which you had thought would be familiar . . . are not familiar at all. Grief can turn a soft memory into an unforgiving rock face or a hairbrush into a sword to pierce the heart. Regrets, like injected foam, expand to fill the space you give them. Words spoken or heard are like an old cassette left next to a magnet – muffled by exposure to greater force.

There is beauty here but it is strange and unnerving. In the end, the only thing which can pass the border controls into this strange new land is the faith which was there before its gates opened. The One who was there on the other side, is here on this side too, as it turns out. God, who created the love which hurts so much, will also give the balm to soothe the rawness of grief. Not today, nor tomorrow, perhaps – but in time.

Early on Monday morning last week, before things began to crumble so dramatically and irreversibly, I took a walk in the frost. The most ordinary things, like a crumpled and discarded bud, were turned into delicate works of art by the icy fingers of winter.

I shall continue to look for beauty in this new winter landscape – and I believe I shall find it.

Of Geese and Sages

I am learning that it is full of surprises, this landscape of grief. Some of its arduous climbs are undulating slopes, and some of its easy vistas are beset by hidden crevasses – just ready to swallow the unwary. At times I like to think I shall swoop across it like the Grey Goose – flying nobly on alone, as if untroubled. Other times I cross it more like a snail – propelled along on a trail of sorrow and a danger to anything that grows!

Sometimes it contains a mirror, this strange landscape – and you catch sight of yourself as you go by. They must be such narrow mirrors though, for they only show one person – never two. Like an inexperienced pilgrim, you ache as you travel here – but mainly in the heart. To experience grief as a physical ache has been a surprise.

And then there are the people you meet along the way. Many of them are unable to speak the language here. Some don't even try; they resort to the universal unspoken gestures of the foreign traveller – a smile, a hug, a tear shed in sympathy. These things are instantly understood, and received with thanks. Others speak as if they have an old phrase book and are urgently thumbing through to find the right page. A bit like the phrase book – you usually know what they mean, even if it ends up sounding slightly off kilter, as if you want to travel by hansom cab or pay for your shopping with doubloons!

Others find themselves in this place promoted to the rank of prophet without ever knowing it. One such was the 6-year-old who presented me with a very special bracelet. At a children's service on Sunday, each child was making an 'advent bracelet' with different coloured beads to represent the different elements of the Christmas story. The idea was that these bracelets should be taken home and used in the weeks leading up to Christmas to retell the story. He came across, sat down next to me and explained that his had another purpose:

> I have made this for you, because you don't have Fiona any more. She has gone to heaven.

I thank God for all the people I am meeting in this strange place – but today I thank him especially for that small prophet.

The Currency of Kindness

It continues to surprise, this land of grief. Its topography is so hard to read – like the shifting sands of the desert. To climb a tiny hill can feel like scaling a mountain – leaving the lungs gasping for air at the top. Once scaled, the view behind may be spectacular, but the view ahead is hidden, at least for now. Some of the valleys which look like no more than a ditch prove to have sides so steep that they all but blot out the light.

As ever with foreign travel, the currency is unfamiliar too. Money has little value. It can pay the bills and provide some distraction, but it has no real worth. After all, it could not pay any fee to prevent crossing the border into here. In this land the currency is kindness. It comes in words and actions, cards and letters, and even smiles.

I started this week by re-reading all the cards and letters which I have received. They came from every direction, in every kind of handwriting and from every age. Some were poetic, some fulsome, some brief – but all have made me richer here.

I thank God for every single one of them. Like money sent home from abroad, they have helped to sustain life in this foreign land and I am humbly grateful.

Invisible Borders

I once heard a refugee describe how the border with his home country ran just alongside his refugee camp. He could stand at the edge of the camp and gaze across at an old familiar tree in the home country – but he could not go there. The border was both invisible and impervious.

I am finding that the landscape of grief has just such a border. I can gaze across it at old familiar things. I can watch normal life unfold before my eyes, and I can stand and have a conversation with those across the border as if nothing separated us. That said – it is impossible to cross for now. When it comes down to it, they live there and I live here and nothing can be done about that. I make occasional forays into their land, and they are precious. It turns out, though, that I take the border with me. I am like a cartoon character racing to outrun an elastic band – legs whirring and arms pumping, but the snap of the elastic must bring me back as surely as night follows day.

The refugee made a new life for himself across the border. He would still gaze from time to time at the old, familiar tree – but he found others in his new home. Like the old one, they provided shade and the kind of mental landmark which makes any new place a little less strange. Today, I shall go looking for trees . . .

Times and Spaces

One of the features of travelling outside your own country is that you find yourself unable to read amounts – be they of money, distance or ingredients. The 'small' pack of a familiar ingredient in a foreign supermarket may be way too big, or the 'large' pack in another may be way too small. Distances can be deceptive too. Two towns which look adjacent on a map may be minutes apart, or hours apart, depending upon the traffic conditions.

I am finding that I am unable to read this particular map. The distance between this task and the next one may appear to be very short, and yet it will take hours, or weeks. The distance from here to the borders of the land where I used to live is one which I cannot begin to calculate.

As ever when staying abroad, shopping can prove to be an interesting experience. Not having the right coin with me, I had to ask a member of staff to release a trolley for me. 'Big or small?' she asked. Momentarily thrown off balance, I reluctantly replied 'small'. In fact, my judgement had been poor, and even the small trolley was too big. I shall have to learn how to shop here, I think.

Border Controls

The further I go into this land of grief, the more I become aware of those things which were removed from me at the border without my knowledge or consent. Somehow at the border, parts of my memories were confiscated. Never the whole of them – but there are patches missing, as if an overzealous border guard has combed through them and left gaps. The patting down of my sense of perspective was a little 'vigorous' too – leaving it misshapen and needing to find its level again – which I have no doubt it will.

Every once in a while, though, I find some little gem here. I turn it over with glee, like finding contraband chocolate smuggled through under the very noses of the border guards. One such is a music box, which I found yesterday. It was presented to Fiona and I on arrival in our first church, newly married. It depicts the two of us, with an unrecognizable amount of hair. With a little persuasion, the figure of me still rotates, slightly wonky, to the tune of 'The Happy Wanderer'. What really made me smile, though, was that in order to take a photo of it, I had to prop the two of us up against one another.

Got that one past customs at the border, didn't I?

Home Comforts

I am finding in this foreign land of grief that occasionally I turn a corner and find a familiar thing, as if transplanted here. It is somehow out of place, like a bright red postbox on a Latin American street, but an equally welcome sight. I stumbled across just such a thing yesterday.

I spent some hours in tearful prayer in the peaceful oasis of Douai Abbey in Woolhampton. With me I took a Bible and a brand-new bound notebook. However, when I opened the notebook, I found a familiar verse printed at the bottom of the first page. It stood there, like a bright red pillar box on a foreign street – a reminder of a more familiar home. This verse had been there when I set out years ago to work with the Belgian Evangelical Mission. When I arrived in the Ardennes to lead a team for the mission, the team accommodation had been stripped bare of every item of furnishing except for . . . this verse framed above the fireplace. When Fiona and I got married, the minister handed us a Bible at the altar as a gift. On the flyleaf he had written . . . this verse. On the morning I moved to my new church here in Newbury, the last thing

I read before my Bible was packed was . . . this verse:

> Be strong and courageous. Do not be afraid;
> do not be discouraged, for the LORD your God
> will be with you wherever you go.
>
> Josh. 1:9

To read this was to remember that this foreign land is foreign only to me. I am no further out of reach here than I was in that other country.

Years ago, some friends of mine were stranded in the far north of Sweden and needing some help. I spoke to a friend in a global mission agency, who spoke to a friend in the Evangelical Alliance who spoke to a friend in the Swedish Evangelical Alliance, who spoke to the pastor of the local church, who was dispatched to visit. Far away was near at hand, it seemed.

This land of grief is disorientating and unfamiliar in so many ways – but it is not out of reach. It has postboxes too, which means that I can always send a card.

Single Ticket

As I continue to live in this new land of grief, I am struck by the parallels with other times when I have stayed away from home. At first, you can be so taken with the novelty of what you see around you that the country you have left behind seems shabby, or dull, or uninteresting by comparison. Stay a little longer, and some of the quirks of what you have left behind assume a kind of rosy glow, making you curious to sample them once again. Stay longer still, and the limitations of the new place may become rather more annoying than the ones you have left behind. In short, it is time to go back.

The comparison is not altogether fair, since the travels I describe above have always been ones I have chosen to undertake. Not so on this occasion. Furthermore, going back is not an option. I cannot go back to where I used to live – my ticket was one way. That is not to say that I am stuck here, though. There is a path – but it lies ahead, rather than behind. I have not been here long enough to discern it yet, but I know that it is 'over there' in Another Place.

Yesterday I paid a visit to Anthony Gormley's artwork of the same name – a place I had last visited with Fiona. The statues still stand there – stock still and staring out to sea. Sometimes they are hidden, sometimes they stand tall – but always they turn their steely gaze to another place.

I was especially struck by one figure. The waves were lapping at his chest, and all but engulfing him. He is unmoved, though – and he continues to look to Another Place. I am hoping that I can do the same . . .

Silent Night

They celebrate Christmas here too, it would seem –
just as they did in the place where I used to live.
To find old traditions here is reassuring. The sound
of familiar carols is good – like a snatch of your
mother tongue heard on a foreign street. Old tastes
and smells are here too – as if imported effortlessly
across the border. When savoured, though,
they turn out to be not quite as you thought.
Sweet tastes turn bitter on the tongue here, and
warming scents can chill the heart. In the midst of
celebrating the presence, an absence stands out all
the more. Chirpy melodies sound shrill, as if played
on a strange instrument for which they were not
written.

And yet, here too I find the fragile baby – all but
alone in a place where he scarcely belongs. He is
loved, of course – even adored. He is cared for and
nurtured – but he does not belong. This is a foreign
place, to which he was propelled by love.

On this silent night, where no greeting can be
exchanged, I am grateful for the presence of One
who did not belong.

365 days

If I am going to be living in this foreign land for some time, then I shall need a calendar. In fact, I already have two – one fat and one thin. The days and dates here are the same as anywhere. There are 365 of them, and they will roll from spring, to summer, to autumn, to winter, with no respect nor pause for sorrow.

Living in a foreign land, though, I am likely to find that the calendar 'milestones' are different – a bit like those foreign bank holidays which commemorate some political figure of whom you have never heard.

Unmarked on any calendar that I can buy here are the anniversaries marked in the heart. They are the anniversaries of engagement, of holidays, of moving here or starting there . . . and even of diagnoses. I could mark these on any calendar in any colour – red, black or blue, but in truth they are marked indelibly on the heart.

More important, then, to mark some new things on the new calendars. I need to write there the things that are done in this foreign land. Where will I go? What dates will I circle with new memories for the calendars for next year and beyond? Right now, that particular pen is too heavy to pick up. The time will come, though, I am sure. Back where I used to live, I learned a song entitled 'I Do Not Know What Lies Ahead' which talked all about God holding the future.

I might just hum it to myself as I fix the calendars up . . .

POSTCARD

11

Out by One Second

There comes a point while living in a foreign country when your description of how long you have been there changes. There comes a point when you stop referring to weeks, or even months – and say instead the year in which you moved there.

In one sense, the passing of a calendar year is an artificial construct – when the clocks tick over from 23:59 to 00:01 in a few hours' time the difference is no more than a matter of minutes. In another sense – it is all the difference in the world. We humans have a need to divide up time in order to make sense of it. Hours, moments, months and years are the cataloguing system in our mental library and we cannot do without them.

From 00:01 tomorrow, it will be last year that I moved to this foreign country. From 00:01 it will be last year that I last held her hand, heard her voice or saw her smile. From 00:01 it will be last year that she died. In truth, those things will be no further from me than they are right now – but they may well feel it.

Right now, my faith in a God who was yesterday, is today, and will be tomorrow matters more than ever.

Home from Home

I am discovering that, no matter how far you travel here, the things you left in that old country are not far away. As I write this, I am more than 3,000 miles from home, enjoying the company of loved ones. The language, and even the alphabet, are different. The skyline is different. Much of the food is different, and the climate is definitely different.

The climate of the heart, though, travels with you. The sun may beat down outside whilst it rains inside, or a wild wind may snatch at the heart and imagination whilst all around the air outside is as still as can be. Sometimes I think the frost of this inner winter is thawing now. Then I catch a glimpse of an old photo or touch a familiar object again and the thermometer plummets.

One day, maybe soon or maybe not, these two climates may equalize, like warming the air up in an aircraft before the pressurised cabin is opened up on a blistering runway. Until then, I shall carry my climate with me, I think.

Between

As I sit and write this now, I am in a busy international airport. It is a bit like Narnia's 'wood between the worlds'[1] – except much less peaceful. Everywhere there are people looking out of place. Some have too many clothes because of where they are going. Others have too few because of where they have been. Some have their precious luggage clingfilm-wrapped and they watch it like hawks. Others have little more than a collection of carrier bags – or alternatively they leave a laptop dangling like a bauble from an unattended trolley.

Some look excited, some look anxious, but everybody looks like they don't belong here – which in truth they don't. That expression – that out-of-sorts, not-quite-belonging, could-we-get-this-over-and-get-somewhere expression is one which I have come to recognize in the mirror these past few weeks. It is the face of a single man – which I have not been for well over thirty years. It is the face of a widower, which surely describes someone other than me? It is the face of a man whose life seems to be as much about what has changed as it is about what remains, at least for now.

In this particular wood-between-the-worlds, with its connections to the wide world, there is just one thing in common amongst all the passengers of different races and backgrounds. They all want to get somewhere. With that, at least, I am familiar. I'm just not quite sure where it is . . .

The Treachery of Absorption

When living away from home, and once you realize that the stay may be long-term, things begin to change. You learn the language. You grow to love the food. You stop scanning the supermarket shelves for those things which you know you can't get here anyway. In short, you learn to fit in. To do so can be quite gratifying – a successful experiment in cultural adaptation. This is not where you meant to be, and it may not have been your choice to come here – but you are making the best of it.

And then, the moment of treachery comes. You are walking through your new-found neighbourhood or talking in your new language with your new friends, when you stumble because you cannot remember the old ones. Perhaps you struggle for a word which was once so familiar on your lips and it just won't come. You're glad the people in that other country can't see you now, because you would feel ashamed.

There are days now, in this land of grief, when I feel like I am starting to fit in. I recognize that single man in the mirror and do not flinch. I look at an old picture in a new space or sit in a new chair in an old room and it feels . . . normal. Then there are other moments when that new normal feels like a treachery to the old. It feels like the person who has studied their new language so hard that when a newspaper comes in their mother tongue they can no longer read it. Absorption, which was such a laudable aim, feels like treachery in that moment.

At least one of the many cards I received on entering this new country quoted this phrase:

> Faith is not knowing what the future holds – but knowing who holds the future.

I was certainly surprised to see it on the side of a burger van in a safari park in the desert! It is, of course, true. However, I am learning that in this place I have to know not only who holds the future, but who holds the past.

Stubborn

I used to think it was an affectation when people kept on using an aeroplane boarding pass stub as a bookmark long after their flight was over. It seemed to be a subtle reminder to everybody else that they were the kind of people who did this so often that they could be nonchalant about it. Maybe there was another, even more subtle message here too. Maybe it was a reminder that they could go just as easily as they had come. Another ticket, another plane, and maybe another book – and they could step right back onto the tarmac where they had begun.

I am holding rather stubbornly to my 'ticket stub' just now. Very soon it will be time to return to work. I shall swap the mental garb of mourning for the working clothes of normality and recover some of the rhythms of life I knew before. Patterns of getting up, getting out, working and returning to the house will settle around me. I can't quite let go of my ticket stub though – not yet. I need some reminder that I am a visitor here. This is not my place. My place is that other one, where the rhythms of my life were syncopated with another's.

I suspect that one day the ticket stub will just fall out whilst I move busily from one task to another. Either that, or I shall swap one book for another and simply forget to transfer it over. One day, that will happen. Not today, though.

Adjustment Fatigue

Yesterday was a good day – infused with the zesty scent of new possibilities and a whole string of new stories to be published. Yesterday was a bad day – stalked by the dank smell of melancholy. Yesterday was a good day – meeting with people who matter in all sorts of ways. Yesterday was a bad day – with fears about tomorrow playing some ghastly version of hide-and-seek amongst the realities of today. Yesterday, like most days in this foreign land, was exhausting.

It is easy to forget that simply living 'abroad' in a place where language and culture and norms do not come naturally, is tiring. Unwittingly, you are engaged in a constant battle to adjust, as if spending your day on a balance ball. Years ago now, I spent a year living abroad and speaking a foreign language nearly all the time. For the first few months, even the very business of living was exhausting. The years have not changed that.

Hopefully, the intervening years have taught me that fatigue cannot be charged, like a bull at a red rag. Nor can it be ignored, like some distant smoke alarm which seems like somebody else's problem. Instead, it must be accommodated, like a creeper growing round the lamppost or a tree growing away from the immovable fence. This, too, is an adjustment – but hopefully it will pay dividends when said tree flourishes.

Alone Together

Sometimes when living in a strange land you find yourself drawn to others who also never expected to be here. Like you, they are out of context and looking for anchors in this alien place. Ten days ago, I met just such a stranger.

Ginny was born in Ireland in 2016, and for some reason found herself without a home. Rounded up and brought across to a small village in West Berkshire, she came into the tender care of the Dogs Trust. It was there that she and I met each other. As a lurcher, she doesn't really have a voice – but her silence spoke to mine. Looking for another breed entirely, I found myself drawn so powerfully to her. Maybe there was a sadness or a wisdom reflected in those amber eyes, or maybe I just fell for the tasselled ears. Either way, I was smitten.

After careful checks by the Dogs Trust, and some trial walks, she has now come to live here with me. These two characters, thrust out of context by circumstances they did not choose, are pooling their resources to forge a new context. She is a little nervous, and I have a lot to learn – but the partnership has so much to offer.

Watch this space . . .

POSTCARD

18

Leave to Remain

If you are going to stay in a foreign land, then the chances are that before too long you will have to work. The time will come when you have to swap 'just arrived' or 'settling in' status for 'one of us' and you may have 'Leave to Remain' stamped in your passport. Today, that day has come for me.

Accompanied by my new companion, I shall head into work and see whether the mantle of 'Baptist minister' still fits about my shoulders. Around me, I have an invisible army of people praying for me. Before me, I have a crowd of lovely people who are ready to welcome me, and within me I have something else – a calling.

Some twenty-six years ago, on the day that I was ordained, the preacher picked up on an obscure text from the Old Testament story of Gideon. Gideon was an unlikely hero who found himself thrust into the limelight to lead a small army to a great victory. The text said the following:

> The Spirit of the LORD clothed Gideon, and he sounded the trumpet . . .
>
> Judg. 6:34, ESV

God had a tune to be played, and a trumpet on which to play it, but the missing piece was a man like Gideon – fearful, unsure and unsteady, but with enough puff to do the job.

In truth, I do not know until I try whether I have 'enough puff to do the job' – but today, I pick up the trumpet.

A Thin Place on a Wintry Hill

Sometimes when living far from home, people will take a little soil from the 'old country' with them. In the new and unfamiliar place, there is then always a connection with the old beneath their feet.

This morning I stood on a windswept slope in West Berkshire, overlooking Watership Down. As the snow blew all around, I laid the ashes of my very best friend to rest. As seasons come and go and the cherry tree planted there begins to flower, she will be especially remembered. It is a 'thin' place – standing in the new but not far from the old. I've a feeling that Ginny and I will often be found there – her quivering with excitement at the scents on the breeze, and me grateful for all the years I had.

On this occasion, nobody else's words would do, so I wrote my own tribute:

You are the crest on a breaking wave
You are the kite wheeling in a golden sky
You are the scrunch of stones washed by the sea
You are the last and hardest steps to see the mountain view
You are the wisdom in the eyes of our sons
You are the courage in their hearts
You are the metre which stops the poem from seeping into prose

You are the note which stands between dissonance
and harmony
You are a chord within my heart, now playing only
half a tune
You are the pause, the breath taken before a foolish
response
You are the rich depth of autumn
The promise of spring
The summer joy of a perfect sky
The welcome nip of a winter's day
You are half of me, and I am half of you
You are, forever, my bravest and best.

Misremembering the Old

Sometimes, when living abroad, even the mediocre things you left behind assume a kind of rosy glow which they never had before. Scented with a whiff of nostalgia, they become better than they ever were.

To be honest, I never really liked Valentine's Day. The choice of cards for a man to give to a woman are frequently daft or rude, and the gifts are overpriced or silly. I shall probably always regret that the last Valentine's gift I bought for Fiona was a fridge magnet saying something like 'I love you even though you steal the duvet'. I would gladly have it stolen 1,000 times over right now! In short, I am not looking forward to Valentine's Day 2018.

For now, I shall simply be grateful to God for the companionship he has provided in this season of turbulent adjustment.

Day 100

In another land or another context, you might expect the 100-day milestone to mark 100 days of the new adventure. In this one, it is quite simply 100 days without her. 100 sunrises, 100 sunsets, 100 unmade cups of tea.

The truth below, written by the apostle Paul, and etched on a rather more tasteful Valentine's gift from years gone by, remains.

Love always hopes.
Love never fails.[1]

A Landscape Transformed

This week it has been snowing in the land where I now live. Snow has a soothing effect on the landscape – like a cool cloth on a fevered brow. Sharp corners are rounded, bare trees are frosted, dropped litter and chewed up verges are hidden by a kind of physical amnesia. Every one of the millions of snowflakes is an emissary in this campaign of transformation. As they fall, drift and settle, between them they contrive to hide what was seen.

New memories and experiences fall in similar fashion upon this landscape of grief. Each one is tiny, and incapable of making the slightest difference on its own. The corners are too sharp, the hollows too deep, the cracks too wide. Between them, though, they begin to transform a landscape. Sometimes now it is possible to look over it and see a little beauty where before there were scars. Sometimes the sun creates more brightness than shadows across it.

Like the snow, though, the transformation can be temporary. Snow does not fill the pothole in the road or round the sharp corner of the roof – it only makes it look that way. With the melt the new becomes old again and the quest for transformation resumes. What I am finding, though, is that even a temporary transformation can be welcome. To see beauty instead of scars, or to see softness instead of hard edges is a sign of hope even when it is ephemeral. The land of grief, like any other land, has seasons . . .

A Song Far from Home

To live in this foreign land and yet still try to sing the song of faith is not a new thing. People of faith were doing it as far back as the sixth century BC when exiles on the bank of the River Tigris tried to remember their spiritual home even though it cost them dear. In Psalm 137, harps hung on a tree and captors smirking at them, they tried to summon up a faith all but quashed by their circumstances.

Today, before a congregation of Christians drawn from every tradition in Newbury, I sought to do the same thing:

> As most of you will know, my wife, Fiona, died in November last year. For the past seven years she had been battling cancer – with multiple surgeries and repeated rounds of chemotherapy. On at least two occasions during that time, bad news was delivered at Easter. On both occasions, it was on a Maundy Thursday.
>
> Last year was no exception. On Maundy Thursday her oncologist finally told us that there was no more which could be done. All curative options had been exhausted. Fiona was handed over to the care of the local Sue Ryder palliative care team – who would see her through to the end.

The next day was Good Friday – and we were both here, along with all of you. After the service, we joined in the walk through town to the Methodist church. When we got there, Fiona had to sit on the wall for the short service in the open air, as she was too weak to stand. This was to be an Easter like no other . . . and our last together.

Two days later, I left the house shortly before seven for the Easter sunrise service. Fiona was really needing her sleep at that time, so I closed the front door very quietly behind me. That was when it struck me with a kind of searing clarity: next year, she will be up before I am at Easter.

There it is – in all its simplicity and depth. What we sing about, what we proclaim in our churches . . . all comes down to this. Do we believe that those who die in Christ are raised to life? I do, and it makes it possible to live in a miasma of constant sadness but with an unshakeable hope. I shall celebrate this Easter without her, but not without hope . . . and on Sunday morning, she will be up before I am.

Not Jumping the Fence

Occasionally in this new land of mine, I catch sight of the suitcases I used to use when travelling. They are far more than I shall ever need for one, and I look wistfully at a sunhat perched on top of them which no one will ever wear again. These are bags for those who travel, not for those who stay.

There are other bags, though, which I have packed many times in these past five months. I pack them in a hurry, like a character in a film storming out of their life and heading for the airport. I pack them as if I have had enough of living in this strange place called grief and I would like to go home, thank you very much. This experiment in living alone has been interesting, and on some days I have survived it better than I thought possible. However, enough is enough, and now it is time to go back to being married, just like I have been for the past thirty years. I crave the easy familiarity of routines honed over the years and a companionship so deep as to be instinctive.

Thoughts trailing like a stray sleeve caught in the suitcase lid, I head for the border of this land and demand to be let through. Sadly, I cannot pass. The border is sealed, the guards are impervious, and my ticket was non-returnable and one way. I live here now. Bag tucked under my arm, I head disconsolately back, and stow it away for next time.

This is a process which is likely to repeat many times, I think – like a dog running time and time again at a high fence before realizing it cannot be jumped. However, as with every trip away from home, it looks slightly different each time you return. Each time I come back from the border with that suitcase, ready to stash it away, I see the house just a little differently. I move things around, I update old things, I act like I am intending to stay here. Like a person with no passport, I start to think how I can make a life here rather than pining for there.

Family are a huge help – constant in their love, and unchanged from the way they were. They live here, as well as there, it turns out. Friends are a blessing – kind, patient, standing by but never pushing in. The value of my faith is incalculable – lending light to the darker days and hope to the deeper valleys. Even if I did not choose to live here, there are ways to make it work and people who are willing to help.

Not ready to pack those 'go-bags' away quite yet – but maybe one day.

Wish You Were Here

Same place.

Same view.

Six months apart.

Worlds of difference.

POSTCARD

26

Home Advice from Abroad

Sometimes shops in holiday resorts would offer postcards with no picture. Instead, the front would contain a checklist of postcard-style information which could be deleted as applicable. This might include:

- ☐ Weather is good/bad/indifferent
- ☐ Food is too spicy/too bland/interesting
- ☐ Hotel is smart/shabby/comfortable

Very soon, I shall have been living here in this land of grief for seven months. This being so, I am sending a list back to that other place. These are lessons learned here which count so very much there.

- ☐ Never believe that money is worth more than time – it is a poor trade.
- ☐ There are many conflicting duties, but the primary call on you is love.
- ☐ The things which have the highest value are those which have no price.
- ☐ A beautiful view shared is a view immeasurably enhanced.
- ☐ It is never too soon to say sorry nor too late to swallow your pride.
- ☐ Every conversation has value, no matter how trivial its content.
- ☐ Faith, hope and love endure, to coin a phrase.

Spring

It was winter when she left. Not a crisp and hopeful winter, full of sparkling promise as it had been the previous day. No, this was a winter day of dwindling light and remorseless rain, streaking the windows and bouncing off the pavements. Colours were insipid, light, muted – as if the day were muffled.

Yesterday was a spring day, apparently. The calendar says that summer is nearly here and everywhere there are splashes of colour, like guests arriving dressed for a party which has not yet begun. Yesterday I visited a special place, my little bit of there which is here. The rain drummed on my coat and the grass squelched beneath my feet. Right there, though, above the spot where she will be forever remembered, her cherry tree was flowering. Some of the bigger flowers had been felled by the rain, unable to resist the onslaught. Some of the newer, tighter buds were holding on, the droplets of water making jewellery out of them.

Showing fragile beauty in the storm and insisting on colour in the drabness seems such a fitting memorial for the bravest and best. Spring is coming.

Blessings and Regrets

One of the features of living unexpectedly here is that you occupy what is now your permanent home country as if it were only temporary. You make only short or mid-term plans, but never long-term ones. You shop erratically, as if not wishing to fill cupboards you might leave behind. You make rapid friendships, as travellers often do. You eat like Moses' Exodus people of old – staff at the ready and more mind on the journey than the plate. You tidy things away in a hurry too.

I have a drawer I am filling with regrets. Some are like a tiny scrap of paper, torn off the bottom of a leaflet. Others are more like essays – filled front and back with tightly packed handwriting. I have been stuffing them in the drawer in such a way that you can squeeze more in, but never open it to take them out. If you try it, the papers curl against the edge of the drawer and it jams half-open – mocking your attempt.

The other day, I shoved a blessing in with the regrets, and now I cannot seem to take it out again. A family with two small children had been to visit me, and I had brought out the big box of Lego we keep for such occasions. I say 'we', but it was her idea to keep it. Thinking ahead, she rescued the box from the charity shop and said we might need it one day – which we did.

When the children had gone, it was time to put the scattered Lego away. Scraping up handfuls and pouring them into the crate, tears fell with the little bricks as I regretted bitterly that she had not heard the children's chuckles of delight.

It was only later that I realized what a blessing it had been to have those children here – filling my all too quiet house with their laughter and noise. Can't get it out of that drawer now, which is annoying.

I really should be more careful where I keep my blessings, so as not to mix them up with the regrets.

A Cross-border Confession

When I used to live in that other place, holidays to France were an annual feature. The rumble of the wheels down the ferry ramp and the first sight of a French flag fluttering over the port always brought a frisson of joy. So, too, did speaking another language. The sheer fact of speaking a different language and saying different things made me feel like a different person. I could say them 'over there' . . .

I am about to write something from 'over here' which I could never have written 'back there'. I could never have written it because it would have been embarrassing and awkward. I would never have written it because it would have been untrue. Nonetheless, I write it now. I am lonely. Married to Fiona for thirty years, and in love with her for longer than that, life without her by my side is shockingly different. One day last week a 24-hour period passed where my only conversations were on the phone or with a cashier at the supermarket. Mine is by no means a unique experience, and I have endured it for a far shorter time than many. All the same, it is a shock to find that it is true.

For those who want to help, I wanted to write a message or two. Firstly – thank you. Your kindness and warmth are a reflection of God's image in the foxed mirror of humanity, and it is wonderful to see.

Secondly, please be assured that my loneliness is neither your problem nor your fault. You did not cause it and I do not count it as your duty to rectify it. Your attempts to distract me from it are always welcome, and the place in your heart from which they come is very dear. Please don't be surprised, though, if I do not always accept them. The reason for my refusal has everything to do with me and nothing to do with you. Part of the collateral damage of bereavement is a wastage of the confidence muscle, if there is such a thing. That muscle which heaved body and soul up over the parapet of home has shrunk, you see. I look out over the threshold of home to a landscape filled with life, laughter, food, drink and conversation, and I both move towards it and quail from it. I will learn, and the muscle will grow back, but it may take a little time.

Thirdly, please don't let the sea mist of sadness which sometimes rolls off me put you off from telling me about your life. I want to know. I want to hear the shrill sound of laughter and the clatter of ordinary dishes and the occasional curse! It reminds me that there is a life out there, beyond the mist – and I still belong to it.

Finally, I may be lonely, but I am not alone. My God is ever with me. His people carry me in their hearts and prayers, which is an act of the truest love. I live here now, but so does God.

Reasonable Adjustment

When you first start to live abroad as a foreigner, people make adjustments. For the most part, they realize that you know things are 'done differently here' and that you might be unaware of the unwritten rules. If your turn up too early or too late; if you wear clothes which are too informal or too smart; if you bring a gift which is inappropriately large or small – people will make allowances. These things are only to be expected from a new resident here.

Throughout the first months of living here, in this land of grief, people have done just that. They have understood if I am a little more cautious or fragile than I used to be. They have accepted that my appetite for change and progress has been muted, as if a taste bud had been removed. They have understood if occasionally the victor in the battle for today's small wins is sorrow rather than strength. To be honest, they understand it still – but I fear the day when they will not. I fear the day when I will do something like a foreigner making a faux pas in an unfamiliar situation and my supply of understanding will have run out. I am grateful that they are more tolerant of me than I am.

Today, I have had cause to rejoice when I look at the difference which has come over my rescue dog, Ginny, in the time she has been with me (134 days).

The caution and timidity have almost gone. The eyes are those of hunter rather than hunted, and the coat bears the gloss of a contented animal. All the same, I sometimes fear that the slack people cut her 'because she is new' will run out one day. Maybe not yet, though . . .

129

Nothing Planned

One of the curious things about living abroad is that the 'obvious' special days, the instinctive milestones on your calendar, mean nothing to anybody here. Days which have formed part of your emotional and psychological landscape for as long as you can remember simply do not feature here. My online calendar reflects exactly that truth today:

For just about all my adult life, this day has been an opportunity to celebrate the difference my beloved Fiona makes to the world. Every birthday present bought, every candle snuffed, every 'happy birthday' sung has allowed us to rejoice that the world has truly been a better place with her in it. Her fierce loyalty, her brilliant mind and her steadfast love have touched our lives in a million untold ways.

Today, she is not here to celebrate. All those benefits linger on, of course – but who feels like celebrating a birthday when the guest of honour is unable to come? Maybe in future years I will find myself able to celebrate this day once again. Maybe it will become a kind of 'Fiona day' to cherish those things which she also cherished. Not this year, though.

This year, I walked with Ginny beside the sparkly sea. This year, I laid a single sunflower on the waves and watched until it was washed from sight. My beloved sunflower stands tall, I know – but not where I can see her.

Stand tall, my love. Happy birthday.

Distant Figures

Years ago, I used to travel once each year to Serbia, where I lectured in a Bible school. I soon realized how fascinated people were to find out about my life back home, and decided to make those conversations easier. I filled a little photo album with pictures of my ordinary life. As well as family, friends and colleagues there were pictures of red postboxes, buses, local shops and even the supermarket where I did my shopping. My Serbian friends loved them, and they led to many an interesting conversation.

If I had moved abroad and kept that album, I wonder how it might have looked a few years down the line? Would the once familiar have looked strange, or quaint, or slightly unbelievable?

As I write this now, I have been twisting the wedding ring on my left hand, and looking at a picture taken on 29 August 1987. In it two figures at the front of St Salvator's Chapel in St Andrews look so very far away. They don't look real to me. In fact, they look rather like the figures of a bride and groom you might stand on the icing of a wedding cake.

They are not. It is my beloved Fiona and I, flanked by her sister on one side and my brother on the other. It was taken just at the moment that we

135

made our wedding vows to each other thirty years and 364 days ago. Like every couple on their wedding day, our heads were filled with dreams of what the future might hold. Many of them came true, and there were many more besides. Others did not, and I have left them on the far shore of that other country.

I shall not blog tomorrow, but today I wanted to thank God for the thirty years that were. Throughout them I was fortunate enough to have a companion whose faith, wit and steadfast love made me whole. For that, I shall always be grateful. God bless you and keep you, my bravest and best.

Far Away Is Near at Hand

As I write this, I am a very long way from home. I am several continents and 4,500 miles away, in fact. Outside in the street are the toots and cries of a busy street in Nepal, and above me tower the mighty Himalayas. All this could hardly be further from my day-to-day life at home. And yet, that other country haunts me here.

For my first few days here, I have been following a path laid down by the inspiration of my bravest and best. I have spoken to teachers and visited schools where money given in her memory has been invested in the lives of Nepali schoolchildren. Their eager faces and enthusiastic learning would have made her glow with pride, I know.

And now, here in the mountains, I find my heart stirred by their quiet majesty. Silently magnificent, they take my breath away, and I cannot help but think how she would have loved them. Wordless, hands clasped, we would have looked at them and treasured the moment. Eleven months ago today, that became impossible – and I choose to believe that there are other mountains for her to see now.

Years ago, on a railway embankment somewhere between Reading and London Paddington there used to be a piece of graffiti which read 'Far away is close at hand in images of elsewhere'. How true that is today.

The Last Postcard?

There comes a point while living abroad, when to continue sending postcards seems a little odd. After all, you live here now. The tastes, sounds and smells are no longer new. The language and customs may still be a little odd – but you can fit in with them to a degree. You live *here*, they live *there*, and if you want to write it should really be a letter rather than a postcard. I am in the process of writing just such a letter now.

The sun has now risen 365 times without its rays ever falling on her face. I have not made her a cup of tea nor held her hand for 365 days. Suns and moons and stars and mistakes and conversations have all passed by without ever sharing them. I have managed, very falteringly, to live without her. She lives *there*, I live *here* and we shall not meet again until I travel to another place more foreign still. It will be foreign to me, I suppose, and yet in the truest sense ever it will be home.

Until that day comes, and today especially – I shall head for the sea. I shall gaze at its seemingly endless waves. I shall look for its invisible far shore, and I shall choose to believe that on another shore she looks for me.

Part Three

Faith and the Land of Grief

4

Battered, Bruised or Shaped?

Faith and the Land of Grief

My father spent all his working life in the timber trade. He started off working with lumberjacks to fell the trees in the forest, went on to work as a 'ganger' loading timber in the East India docks, and ended up as Company Secretary and Personnel Manager of a builders' merchant. We could not go on a country walk without stopping to look at the stump of a felled tree. He taught us how to count the rings so as to find out the age of the tree. He taught us to 'read' the rings too – the fat ones denoting a good year with plenty of rain, and the thin ones denoting a hot, dry year with little growth.

Sadly, his attempts to pass on to me his considerable skills with woodworking failed spectacularly. I have none of his precise skills and patient craftsmanship to show for it. However, what he did teach me was that wood is a living thing. Even once felled, planed, cut and joined into a piece of furniture, it continues to change over time. The atmosphere in a house will darken wood as it dries. The touch of human hands will also affect its hue, bringing about that distinctive patina of which antiques' experts are so fond. Cut wood may be static, but it is not unchanging. I am finding that the same thing is true of theology.

My theological certainties have been placed in a room with open fires since my bereavement. The soot and dust of this emotional reality has settled upon them. I have leaned more often upon them, running my hand along their lines and leaving a trace of sweat and grief behind. My theology bears the patina born of a friction between the soft wood of faith and the hard reality of life. Rather like an antique with patination – this has not diminished its value, but increased it.

Tenets of my Christian faith which I have always held, I hold tighter now. The promises of God are like stakes driven into the ground to hold up the structure of my faith. They are driven further in now, and can withstand stronger winds when they blow. During the course of writing this book, I made a trip to Nepal to visit an educational project supported in Fiona's name. In Kathmandu, the Himalayas were invisible, though their foothills could sometimes be seen through the haze of pollution. Travelling a day's journey away from the city, we arrived in the Middle Hills – much closer to the mountains. On arrival, there was no sight of them. Waking early the next morning, just about the time of the sunrise, I gasped as I looked out of the window and saw them in all their majesty. The sun travelled across them, one by one, lighting up each peak as it went.

Another hour later, and the clouds had stolen them from view. They were still there, of course – but I had a hard time persuading my travelling companions of that fact when they could not see them! The theological truths which underpin my faith are a bit like those mountains – still there but sometimes hidden. If anything, this particular storm has blown the clouds away, rather than gathering them.

Hope is a different colour

When I was very new to the Christian faith, I used to attend a Crusaders' group (now Urban Saints). After attending for ten weeks in a row, I was proudly awarded my crusader badge with its sword, its crown, its shield and its cross. In those early teenage years, I was taught the Hebrews verse that 'faith is confidence in what we hope for and assurance about what we do not see' (Heb. 11:1). At the time, my challenges were only small ones. I had a few friends who would mock my Christian faith at school and I ran the usual teenage gamut of emotional turmoil. However, it was not until that wet November day when Fiona died in my arms that I would fully appreciate what that verse meant.

When such a traumatic thing happens, there is no time for reflection – only instinct. As she drew her last breath, I found instinctively that I knew she was drawing her first breath in heaven at precisely that moment. This was not a courageous thing to say or think. There was no higher reasoning at work which determined that this was the kind of thing a Christian minister ought to think. In that second, with every fibre of my being, I knew it to be true.

It did nothing to detract from the devastating sadness, of course. Moments later the tears would flow as all the regrets about things unsaid and opportunities un-seized would come crashing in on me. It would be then, and on many subsequent occasions, as if I found my-self suddenly beneath a waterfall of sorrow and regret. That said, in the actual moment of indescribable loss my conviction about the reality of Christian hope was more robust and certain than it has ever been. As the writer to the Hebrews, once again, puts it:

> We have this hope as an anchor
> for the soul, firm and secure.

(Heb. 6:19a)

Until that moment came, I would have believed it impossible to hold unquenchable sadness and inextinguishable hope at the same time. Surely, the one would extinguish the other, like trying to hold a lit candle and a jet of water in the same hand? I am still not sure how it works, but I know that it does.

I had talked so much about hope in previous years. I had talked about it in sermons, written about it in books, described it in worship and alluded to it at funerals. Now, though, it was coming home to roost. I feel now more than ever that hope must either be able to withstand the white heat of human loss and sadness or it is not hope at all. On one occasion when I talked about these experiences on the radio, a listener wrote in to ask exactly what sort of hope I was describing. He wanted to know whether it was specifically the hope of being reunited with someone I have lost or some other kind of hope. I feel as if it is both. The hope of being reunited is perhaps the layer which is nearest the surface. It has an immediacy about it which soothes the rawness of loss and grief, especially in the early days. To see the empty chair unoccupied, or an old familiar coat hanging unworn in the cupboard is deeply painful. Countering it with the thought that one day you will see the occupant of the chair or the wearer of the coat again is a real help.

However, deeper down in some sub-strata of faith, there is another layer to hope. It feels now like a fundamental conviction that it has all been 'worth it'. It is no accident that the reference to 'hope' in Hebrews above comes in a letter addressed to those who had risked everything they held dear for their loyalty to Jesus. Their place in society, their acceptance in their own families, and in some instances their very lives were in jeopardy because of their beliefs. Hope, to them, meant the conviction that they had made the right decision and followed the right path. In my understanding of hope now, there is a high melody played by a flute which evokes the face, the laugh and the sight of the one I have lost. That floating melody reminds me that I shall see her again. Beneath it, though, there is a much deeper chord made up of bass notes. I hear it now on a mellow bassoon. This chord is the hope that a lifetime's decision to follow a God whom I cannot see and a Jesus whom I have yet to see has been the right thing to do.

When I came for my 'trial weekend' to my current church, one of the teenagers here put me on the spot by asking me, 'What colour is your faith?' I wonder how you would have replied to that question? It certainly put me on my mettle. In the end, I replied that my faith was probably white – so that it would reflect the colours of what was going on around about it at the time. Looking back, I feel quite pleased with it as an answer given to an unexpected question on the spot. Clever though it may be, it rather dodges the question. What colour is faith, or indeed hope, really? Hitherto, I would probably have thought of it as yellow. After all, yellow is the colour of sunshine, daffodils, sunflowers and the thrusting energy of summer.

Now, I am not so sure. I think I would probably describe it as grey – which is not as dull as it sounds. When I first started to learn watercolour painting, I found that one of the hardest tones to master was grey. A grey can have a bluish tint, like distant hills receding from the viewer through aerial perspective. It can have a warm ochre like Cotswold stone bathed in sunshine. It can have a green hue as it reflects the trees and grass growing beside an old stone wall. Grey is the subtle shade upon which so much of the painting's narrative may be reflected. Even so, is my Christian hope. Some days it has a warmth about it – like sun on Cotswold stone. Other days there is an icy certainty about it – like the mass of a mountain soaring up above mist, cloud and fog.

Perspective is different

It is not only the colour of my hope which is different. My sense of perspective has altered too, albeit not in the way I would have anticipated. Having observed bereavement, and especially early bereavement, in others, I had expected a quickening of my pace. I had expected this summary separation to bring about a kind of urgency. Once the initial seismic shocks of pain and sadness had subsided, I was anticipating a kind of breathless demand to get things done and not to waste another second. Every death, after all, is a reminder of our mortality. We have only so many years and so many opportunities to embrace the love of God before our time runs out.

As a minister of the gospel, I anticipated that I would return to my ministry with a fiery urgency born of my shocking reminder that life is short. I would speak up, speak out and preach up on every occasion. As a naturally driven and energetic person in a job where the work can never be said to be done, busyness is my default setting. Bouncing back, or even crawling back from bereavement, this would surely be multiplied several-fold?

In fact, I have found the opposite to be true. I now feel deeply convicted that life is too short to waste it on the wrong things. I move slower, think longer, listen deeper and talk more often. The tyranny of the to-do list has been replaced with the sanctity of presence. If I get to have one conversation whilst leaving one item on my task list unticked, then I regard that as a fair exchange. Things undone bother me far less than things unsaid or needs unheard. I am not quite ready to abandon my watch and give up on any sense of time, but occasionally it has come close.

To operate in this way runs counter to the way I have been all my professional life. I have always wanted to be busy, and usually have several projects on the go at once. Times without number I would walk home from church, exhausted after preaching at that day's services – with my mind already racing onto the next ones. To find myself no longer that way has been something of a shock, and it is not altogether easy to pin down what has happened. Beneath it all, I think, is a sense of regret. There is not a day goes by when I do not think of a conversation I should have had with Fiona. I deeply regret, too, the times when I invested my energy in sorting things out for her when she was incapacitated, instead of simply sitting with her as life ebbed away. I cannot change it now. However, I can allow it to infuse my sense of ongoing priorities, and I intend to do so.

Having said that, I find that in my preaching ministry I am more able and willing to tackle spiritual inertia than I have ever been before. With the clock forever ticking, there is no time to repent *tomorrow*, or embrace salvation *tomorrow*, or mend a broken relationship *tomorrow*. In 2 Corinthians 6:2 (ESV) Paul says that 'now is the day of salvation' – and I find myself saying so more and more.

Courage is awoken

If death is indeed the last enemy, then maybe every foe after that is somehow diminished – like a pantomime villain trying to scare the children whilst all the while his mask is slipping. Some years ago I had a conversation with a foreman on a building site. We were talking about the difficult conversations he sometimes has to conduct when a worker is not doing their job properly, and has to be told to sharpen up or leave. He told me that after going home and telling his daughters that their mum had died of cancer, no conversation could ever be *that* hard again. I have some understanding now of what he meant.

To say that I have no fears would be false. However, I have found myself better able to face them. In the face of such a great loss, they all take on a different dimension.

When anticipating a meeting where people are liable to disagree with me, or chairing a church meeting where strong and divergent opinions will be expressed, I still take a very deep breath. Nonetheless, I know that, to coin a phrase, 'nobody dies'. Disagreements are costly and awkward and uncomfortable – but ultimately they do not cost us our lives. Rightly handled, they can bring healing rather than harm.

I find a greater courage, too, to challenge those things which may undermine the work of God's kingdom. A careless phrase or an unwarranted criticism of another Christian is something which I might have casually ignored before. I lacked the stomach to challenge it. Now, though, I am more inclined to take the deep breath and to do so. I have seen the value of holding a Christian faith to the very end, and I don't want to see anyone knocked off that particular course unnecessarily.

Calling a halt is something I am also more prepared to do. The email does not have to be answered *now*. The decision on church programme or budget or strategy does not have to be made *now*. The phone call does not have to be returned *now*. With all my emotions now more acutely active than they have ever been before, I am aware that there are times when they can intrude on a decision as much as they inform it. These are not delays born of laziness or fear, but a decision to let the barometer settle before reading the weather of this particular moment.

Aware of all the changes which have gone on in me, and how deeply my own faith has been tested, I am a little more inclined to ask the deeper questions too. I want to know why a person is behaving like *this*, or why a particular event is making the church feel like *that*. To ask those questions does not necessarily mean that any different course of action will be taken, but the same one may be taken differently. People are complex, and their lives contain all manner of complications of which both we and they are scarcely aware.

Pastoring, as I do now, from this different perspective, I like to think that I tread a little more carefully. I walk, rather than running – and even when I walk I look where I put my feet. Like an astronaut on the moon, each footstep is placed more carefully now – testing what lies beneath the surface before putting weight on it.

Conversational theology

Preaching will always be fundamental to what I do as a minister. I have always found it to be a place where

I can use those skills which God has given me. It is a place where I can watch his power at work using the ordinary words of an ordinary person to bring extraordinary transformation. That will not change any time soon. However, I find myself given more and more opportunities for what I might call 'conversational theology'. Unlike the pulpit, which is one to many, these are one-to-one. Unlike a sermon, these are nether scripted nor planned. I am in charge of them only to the extent that I choose my own answers and ask my own questions. Beyond that, these theological encounters may go in any direction which the other party may choose.

I am more at ease with these than I used to be, because the last months of Fiona's life taught me more about the value of conversation than I had learned in all my years up to that point. When physical capacities shrink, and the opportunities for diversions outside the house are removed, conversation becomes a gift from one human being to another. We talked in the car, we talked at the bedside. We talked in hospital corridors and by hospital beds. We talked in hushed tones so as not to disturb others. We talked louder over the hum of the oxygen machine at home. We talked of this, that, the other and everything in-between. When the end came, and the last few hours disappeared down a whirlpool of pain and semi-consciousness, the loss of the ability to talk to each other was the cruellest blow.

So long as I have that ability now – especially with others whose faith may be struggling, or weak . . . or undiscovered, I will seize it. I have to accept, of course, that the theological conclusion of such a conversation is nowhere near as predictable as a sermon. Often a worship leader has asked me ahead of a church service where I am 'heading' with the sermon, and I have always been able to tell them. I cannot do that with these conversations – but it really does not trouble me as it might once have done.

As often as I can now, I have these earnest conversations on the move. Wherever possible, this is 'ambulatory theology' – the conversation taking its course as the feet of the participants do the same. As I have discussed in *Journey: The Way of the Disciple*,[1] walking pace often matches thinking pace. To discuss the things which matter whilst on the move may allow both words and thoughts to run more freely. The last stages of my journey with Fiona by my side taught me the value of discussing the things which matter 'on the way'. Maybe in rediscovering this in my ministry I am returning to old Baptist roots? Many Baptist churches would have a church covenant to 'walk together' and to 'watch over one another'. In this, later, chapter of my life and ministry I am discovering the value of doing just that all over again.

There is a much younger version of myself which would read the words above and stamp his foot with indignation as he told me off for 'selling out' to liberalism. His face growing ever redder with frustration, he would tell me that bereavement was no excuse for 'going soft' and that all the old certainties should remain the same. I've found that if I listen to the voices of the troubled doubter and the earnest seeker, they soon drown out the sound of that angry young man. The walk of faith is just that – a walk, of faith. As a walk, it may take you to places you would not visit if you were travelling on a straight railway track or soaring above in a plane. Driven by faith, there is no telling where it goes, only a certainty about who travels it with you.

5

The Word and the Tree

As I write, I have turned back to the flyleaf of the Bible from which I have been quoting all along. It was presented to Fiona and I on our wedding day by the minister who married us. Standing at the front of St Salvator's Chapel in St Andrews, he placed it in my hands and it has been with us ever since. It has moved from house to house and church to church along the way. Inside, just above the date, '29th August 1987', he has written:

> Be strong and courageous.
> Do not be afraid; do not be discouraged, for the LORD your God will be with you wherever you go.
> Josh. 1:9

Those words have proved to be true. If it were up to me, I would probably not have chosen some of the places caught up in the phrase 'wherever you go'. The valleys have been darker, the mountains steeper, the deserts harsher and the cold plains more bitter than I would ever have anticipated. And yet, through it all, God's presence has brought an incomprehensible strength. Like Joshua and his fellow travellers to the promised land – I am getting there, by the grace of God.

On the last day that Fiona was with me, I went out early in the morning to admire the frost on Greenham Common. Every plant and bush bore traces of it – beautiful in the harsh cold of a winter's morning. I paused then, as I have done many times since, to admire one very special tree. At some point in its life, it has been all but uprooted, and its trunk lies parallel to the ground. With roots partly exposed, and trunk on the ground where the grass grows, this tree has taken a severe knock. The thing is – it is still growing. From that horizontal trunk, boughs, branches and twigs have grown. As the seasons come and go the leaves spread just like any other tree. It is knocked down, but very definitely not knocked out. I have named it 'The Courage Tree', and I never go to the common without stopping to look at it. I hope that I can be like that tree – bowed but not broken, and damaged but growing still.

If reading this book enables you to do the same – then perhaps another courage tree is springing up.

Part Four

Resources for the Traveller in the Land of Grief

6

Survival Tips

Resources for the Traveller in the Land of Grief

As a pastor, I have observed human grief in its many stages and guises. Sometimes you see it before the person dies, especially when they are suffering from a chronic illness. They grieve for themselves, too – as the circle of possibilities within their own life begins to shrink. It may start with the necessity to leave work, followed by the inability to drive, and then the withdrawing from much beloved church or voluntary activities. As a pastor, I have accompanied them often on the journey through those shrinking circles.

Sometimes I have been there in the first few raw moments immediately after a death has occurred. I was a new apprentice pastor, scarcely out of college, when I found myself in the house as an elderly man in the congregation slipped away. Maybe seeing the aura of shock around me, the nurse who came to check and destroy his medications took me under her wing. When she asked me 'Have you ever seen a dead body before?' I shook my head – and she took me into the room with her so that I did not have to do it alone. Years later, and two churches further down the road, I sat in the room with a young couple whose baby had been born far too premature to sustain life. His little, crumpled form was in there with them. I know now that there is an uncanny stillness about such a room, as if a vacuum has been somehow created. The physical presence of a body still recognizable but devoid of life feels like some mocking rebuke of all that has been. Often people don't know whether to cling on, to look away, or to stare off out of the window at a world seemingly unmoved.

After that moment comes the flurry of arrangements to be made, when I can stand slightly apart and act as facilitator. Simply by listening to a life story told in snatches and anecdotes, I can act as the catalyst for the beginning of a grief journey. I ask for these stories because I need to know them in the preparation of the funeral. In truth, though, they need to tell them too. Practical arrangements for a funeral so often bring out other things – old tensions, treasured memories and tales long untold. It is at this stage that I have often been surprised by the physicality of how people do their grieving. On one occasion I had a family who wanted to have their uncle buried in a particular plot so that he could 'see' his old shop from the grave.

On the day of the funeral itself, it falls to me to 'play the professional', putting my own feelings on one side so that I can help others to grieve. My key aim on such occasions is to ensure that any goodbyes are made with dignity and honour. There are certain things which must be said and done, but beyond that I try my best to make it as personal and as warmly human as I possibly can. For the most part, professionalism kicks in at this point, allowing the suspension of my own emotion. For the duration of the funeral, I am 'the minister' and I am required to act as such. My lack of emotion lends strength to those who are at the mercy of theirs. On one occasion I can remember maintaining my composure all the way through the burial of a tiny two-day old baby. I bit my lip as I watched the tiny coffin lowered into the ground, and spoke words of comfort and faith for the mourners gathered round. It was only when I got to the car that my composure deserted me and I had to let the tears flow before I started the engine and drove to the family's house.

With the funeral done and the family scattered to their own homes, my role switches again. Early post-funeral visits may be taken up with discussing the funeral itself, looking at messages received on the day, or helping with any lingering practical details. After that, conversations may move to the new chapters of the mourner's life, and how things will change. Often we will look at a photo on a mantlepiece or a coffee table and we will talk about the one who smiles out at us from it. Over the months those conversations become more wistful as the rawness of loss begins to subside. That person is never forgotten, but they accommodate a different space in the world of the one to whom they are lost.

Having been both an observer and a participant in all the stages above, I would have thought myself to be better prepared for my own grieving. Surely, having watched the grieving process all the way through from early diagnosis, to last days and beyond, I should have been ready? Surely, having accompanied widows and widowers along the rocky path of early loss, catching them when they stumbled and picking them up when they fell, I should have been somehow inured? In fact, I was not.

Often in the weeks leading up to Fiona's death, she would encourage me to get out on my beloved road bike, saying that the physical fitness would help the emotional fitness when the time came. In that, she was right, but I was to find that the shape of my grieving took me altogether by surprise. No two griefs are the same, and even when different people grieve for the same person, they do it differently. Truth to tell, I was a fool to think that my prior professional experience would somehow protect me from my personal loss. The armour I had worn as a professional on the battlefield of grief was useless to me when the sword which struck me was inside. That armour, now, was made of a material so thin that the rapier point of loss sliced through it instantly. I would grieve as husband and lover, not pastor.

The observations below are purely my own, and not intended as normative in any way. However, perhaps the honesty will help for some.

Physics

Years ago, when 'mixtapes' were a thing, I had one with a Bonnie Tyler song on it entitled 'It's a Heartache'. Whilst I liked the song, I thought the very idea of loss as a physical ache was a piece of whimsical nonsense reserved for songwriters and poets. How wrong I was! When Fiona died, I was expecting the tears and the bleakness. I was expecting the fragile emotions and the involuntary shock of inanimate objects suffused with her presence and our memories. I had observed this so many times with other people. Often they would talk about how a song on the radio, a scent in the air, or even an advert on the side of a bus would set them off. I knew about these things, and I was expecting them.

What I was not expecting was to experience my loss as an actual, physical ache somewhere in the middle of my chest. For those first few weeks it was my constant companion – waking and sleeping, in the house and out. The pain would come and go, and was often at its worst as the light began to fade early in the afternoons when I was alone in the house. On those short winter days, I seemed to have developed an emotional clock whose alarm would go off as the darkness drew in. Many days would find me going out to the shops for the second or third time that day, just to distract myself from the pain. This took me altogether by surprise.

Of equal surprise was the fact that I found my emotional state often required a physical solution. When sadness got the better of me, when the walls closed in and the tears started to tear at me, the very best thing was to walk. I walked slowly, I walked fast. I walked before sunrise and after dark. I walked the streets, I walked the parks, I walked the hills. The medicine for which I reached to heal my emotional pain was my walking shoes. Every time, without exception, it helped. It probably helped in other ways too. Grief is an attack on the whole of our being – emotional, spiritual and physical. Inevitably, the consequences of such a wholesale attack are multiple. Amongst the physical consequences are insomnia and lack of appetite. My insatiable need to walk seemed to help with both. Three months after Fiona died, as you will have read in the postcard 'Alone Together', I adopted a rescue dog – Ginny. With her long legs and her muscular build, she needs to be walked at least twice a day, and she is probably grateful that I had set such good habits ahead of her arrival.

There was another aspect to this physical grieving which was equally unexpected. Two months after Fiona's funeral, I buried her ashes beneath a cherry tree in a beautiful green cemetery overlooking Berkshire's Watership Down and Coombe Gibbet. It is a lovely spot, and over the next half century it will begin to develop into a mature woodland, suffused with the memories of all whose remains lie there. What has surprised me is how often I have found it necessary and helpful to visit that cherry tree. Each time I go away to the seaside I bring back a shell or a pebble and place it on the grave as a marker. Often I will sit on the soft grass by the tree, my dog at my side, and cry and pray with the most tremendous sense of connection. These are the kind of things I would expect someone else to do – and yet they have proved helpful to me.

The shock of the ordinary

When you lose someone with whom you have spent all your adult life, there are so many things which you expect to be difficult. You flinch from the birthdays and anniversaries as they roll towards you with all the certainty of an oncoming train. You know that a scarf or a letter or an old photograph found in the back of a drawer will pierce you to the very heart. People handle this in different ways. Some people take the conscious decision to get rid of everything which belonged to the person they loved – from clothes and ornaments to cards and letters. It is not because they don't love them, but because they do. They know that looking at these things will simply be too painful. Others gather up all the belongings of the one they have lost, and put them in a particular room or cupboard. That way, they are still there for those moments when they *choose* to be reminded or *desire* to plunge back into the memories. Others simply leave things where they are, to be 'discovered' as and when. I did this, and accepted as a consequence that there would be times when I stumbled across things in the house which would upset me. To this extent, the house was a 'dangerous' place – full of pitfalls. I thought I would be safe in the supermarket, though – which proved to be wrong.

After Fiona's funeral was done, and the family had all returned to their own lives, I started to settle into my own new one. I had fully anticipated the shock of my first return to the house on my own, and took steps to ease myself into it. However, I had not thought about the shopping. The first time I went to the supermarket, I did what I thought was the sensible thing and chose the smaller version of the shopping trolley. However, when I got three-quarters of the way through my shop for one, and realized that even that small trolley was far too big, the tears came, right there in the aisle. It was not a good moment.

There were other moments, too, when the ordinary seemed to have the power to inflict *extraordinary* anguish. I found that both living room and the bedroom seemed too big. The physical limitations for Fiona in the last few months of her life meant that these were the spaces we had shared more than any other. Now, I could not stand them. Like a wounded animal, I craved small spaces. I avoided the living room unless I had people with me. If I wanted to watch TV, I did it on a tablet balanced on my knee in another room. Meanwhile, in my bedroom, I added a bookcase to the pleasantly uncluttered space specifically because I wanted it to feel smaller. Even when I started using the living room once

173

again, I added a coffee table so as to fill the empty space in the middle.

Even as I write this down, it seems bizarre, and yet it was so. Much as I had experienced the physical shock of grief within my own body – so I was experiencing it in my home environment too. Just as physical objects are suffused with the presence and touch of those who selected and arranged them – so they may also express that person's absence. A home once filled with Fiona's touch now seemed filled with her absence. I find that Christians often berate themselves for some lack of spirituality when physical things have such an effect on them. It is as if they feel they should be capable of rising above such things. I cannot agree. The presence of a physically incarnated Jesus is a reminder that the spiritual inhabits the physical, rather than opposing it. It was in this painfully physical space that I would find new theological insight which I could not have found elsewhere.

Unwelcome blandness

I have always been the cook of our household. Fiona was quite prepared to cook, but did not enjoy it. I, on the other hand, enjoyed it, and so it fell to me. In my first few weeks on my own, I made some small changes to the kitchen. One of them was to buy a spice rack so as to organize my herbs and spices a little better. When I took it out of the box, I was delighted to find that my spice rack came fully charged with twenty-six little jars of herbs and spices. I had never heard of some of them, and couldn't wait to try them out.

However, there was a problem. As time went by, I found that food eaten alone had no flavour of any kind. I could have shaken every little jar from that rack onto my food, and it would still have tasted insipid and un-appetizing. In the last few weeks of Fiona's life, even when it was agonizing for her to do so, we would sit for a few moments together each day at the table for a meal. Even if she could manage only a few mouthfuls, it was a precious shared moment. Sitting there alone now, I found that I could not care less about what was on my plate. Years ago, science fiction films used to portray a future where a meal would be little more than a sweet or savoury vitamin pill dispensed onto a plate. I would not really have cared if it were so.

Of course, I know I have to eat – and will always do so to keep body and soul together. For me, the only thing has been to acknowledge the problem and try to work around it. I try cooking different things which I have not cooked before. I eat at different times, since I only have my own needs to accommodate. Whenever the weather is nice enough, I try to eat outside. I find any and every excuse to bake for others, since this restores the joy of cooking to me.

There is one other thing I have tried too. It used to be a habit of Fiona's and mine to take photos of the view whenever we ate at a café or restaurant abroad. I have a whole collection peeking out from under awnings at a French street scene, a Breton coastline or an Italian lake. Occasionally I will bring one of those photos up on computer or tablet and prop it in front of my place at the table. If the food doesn't taste up to much – at least I can improve the view!

Company

As a pastor, I spend a lot of my time in the company of other people. Some of it is spent teaching or training, some comforting and encouraging, and other times simply working alongside them. I like to think that I function pretty well in the company of others. Somebody wrote to me from a church small group. They had been discussing the story of Jesus' conversation with the woman at the well in John 4:1–26. They noted that it would have been shocking at the time for Jesus to be seen talking to a Samaritan woman, of all people. When they tried to imagine any person to whom they would have been shocked to see me talking – they struggled. This reassured me hugely, I have to say. Basically, I like people and I like to be around them. All this means that I found it a rude shock to discover that my 'confidence muscle' had wasted so much with the experience of grieving that I had lost my appetite for human company.

Often in the first few months of being alone, people would invite me out for a coffee, a drink or a meal. It was all well-intentioned, and they were kind to do it. However, times without number I would find myself flinching at the very thought. Over the course of thirty years, I had learned to navigate my way through many social contexts with Fiona at my side. Facing them alone now, I felt uncharacteristically shy, inept and fearful. What would I say? Who would I sit with? How would I know when to arrive, and more importantly – when to leave? It was as if my 'confidence muscle', if there were such a thing, had wasted away. Oddly, this never oc-curred in a work context, where my purpose for being there was clear. It was only in a social setting that I felt an inability to navigate the expectations.

A wise friend, whose grieving began two years before mine when she lost her husband, said the following to me: 'Don't accept every invitation, but don't reject every one, either.' It was good advice. Whilst the unexpected loss of confidence is awkward and shocking, it does not do to yield to it completely. Instead, a gradual return to social life is important. However, it is good to exercise some caution. I found that I needed to accept that this would be a gradual process – not moving from where I was now to where I once had been instantly. Like learning to walk after an injury, I would have to begin with small steps on level ground. Not only that, but I would have to have a clear plan about how long I was intending to stay and an 'exit strategy' when needed. To start with, the return to any kind of social life has to begin with the people who feed you, rather than drain you. Of course, as a pastor, I am meant to get along with everybody. However, we all know that we find some people easier than others – and early grieving is definitely a time to pick and choose.

Isolation is a mirage in the desert of bereavement – offering replenishment and refuge where it is not to be found. In my bereavement, I found myself often slinking away to be in my own company. My home, altered and difficult as it was, nonetheless offered me a sanctuary where I had no one to oblige but myself. Within its walls I could cry if I needed to, with no one rushing to comfort. I could pick up the old familiar things and handle them with reverent care like the priceless artefacts which they had become. I could laugh, cry, sulk or sleep just as I wanted to. In the end, though, just like the mirage – there was no water here to slake my thirst.

On saying no

It turns out that what I have termed the 'wastage of the confidence muscle' applies not only to personal, but also to professional life. In the first few weeks back at work, I was shocked by my own lack of physical capacity. Often a little time in the office and one meeting in a day would be as much as I could do. This frustrated me beyond measure, as it was not a version of me which I recognized. Not only that, but it was accompanied by an entirely unfounded paranoia that people would judge me for being lazy, or weak, or both.

Even once that crushing fatigue began to recede, I found that nonetheless my capacity for work had considerably reduced. A few months in after my bereavement leave, I found myself increasingly able to fulfil the 'ordinary' and predictable elements of my job. However, the prospect of adding in anything extra was more than I could contemplate. A 'safe' day, in which I knew what was planned and did neither more nor less, was fine. The addition of anything unpredictable, though, sent my levels of energy and enthusiasm plummeting downwards. Unfortunately, my job often includes the unpredictable! In years gone by, the ability to 'debrief' on an unexpected challenge, or to unpack the rigours of an especially demanding day had done more to strengthen me than I had ever realized. Without Fiona, whom I always referred to as my 'bravest and best' by my side, my ability to face such days was massively reduced.

For the past fifteen to twenty years, I have combined local church ministry with other, wider ministries. Some of these have involved writing and broadcasting, and others have involved preaching and teaching elsewhere. I have always found the latter to be stimulating and fulfilling. To teach preaching skills to others and see them discover and hone their gifts has been a real pleasure. Even when it involved marking forty or fifty assignments afterwards, the joy of seeing students discover their latent gifts made it worthwhile. I always enjoyed preaching away from home too. 'Stepping into' an unknown situation and bringing a word from God to bear was a huge privilege and a great joy to me. Preaching in a 'residential' context too, where people are learning together away from home, has been great fun. To provide the teaching at an awayday or a house party has played to my strengths and given me great encouragement. Now, however, I find myself avoiding such things.

In the first year of my bereavement, I have turned down more invitations to speak than at any point in my professional life to date. Things which I have always enjoyed, such as preaching at other churches, lecturing on preaching or leading house parties have simply seemed too much. Even if I had the capacity to do them, I no longer have the appetite. The energy required, and the kind of vulnerability and honesty which makes a good teacher are beyond me. I have no doubt that will change – but for now it remains so.

The shrinkage of the confidence muscle shows especially on the exposed battlefield of leadership. Whilst Fiona and I never made church leadership decisions together, I derived more strength than I shall ever know from her unflinching support. 'Going out on a limb' is so much easier when someone is watching you lovingly from the point where it splits from the trunk. Other pastors who have been similarly bereaved have warned me that I should not expect this to change any time soon. The fact is that we learn how two become one in marriage – sharing secrets, hopes, dreams and aspirations. We learn how to handle the blows together and how to bring the best out of each other. Those habits, which took many years to learn, cannot be unlearned so quickly.

Oddly, I have found the whole process of declining invitations to be curiously liberating. I have never been good at saying 'no' and exercising my right to do so just now has been something of a novelty. On those occasions when I have declined an interesting invitation to speak, I have felt no regret – just a sense of reassurance that now is not the time.

Cathartic confrontation

Sometimes people talk about 'grief work' as if it is a job which simply has to be done. I have always felt it to be an odd description, as it seems an angular phrase for something so nuanced. However, I have been finding that there are some things which you just have to do. They will not go away or reduce until you confront them. This may be the tidying out of a cupboard, the reading of a bunch of letters, or delving into a box of old photos.

One particular instance comes especially to mind. Fiona died in early November, and the following month it was time to clear the decks and make space for Christmas cards in the house. I took the old calendar down off the wall, and walked to the front door ready to put it in the dustbin outside. Hesitating, with my hand on the door knob, I turned back, and brought the calendar back to my armchair. With a deep breath, I worked through it week by week. As the pages turned, all the increasing number of Fiona's medical appointments went before my eyes. As the year went on they got more and more frequent . . . until they stopped abruptly. As you can imagine, it was a tearful read. However, for me, it was a necessary one. If the dustmen had taken that calendar away without my ever having looked through it, I think I would have regretted it. Returning from the dustbin in the drive, and hoping that my red eyes could not be seen from the road, I felt that I had done something important.

Meet the triplets

When you lose the person you love, the circle around the two of you shrinks during the last days. For the person who is ill, colleagues and those associated with a former working life are long gone. Once the horizon shrinks to the physical borders of the home, fewer and fewer people come. Distant friends feel it is intrusive to visit, and even close friends can find the pressure to say or do the right thing so intimidating that they are unsure whether to call in or not. Distant family may visit, but as the sickness grows, and the weakness grows alongside it, only closer family remain. By the time Fiona died on that soggy November day, the circle was a small one.

Having said that, I was pleased to find that in the days immediately following her death it was not as empty as I had thought. Friends and neighbours were near. My church people were constant and thoughtful in their kindness. Friends from chapters of life long gone by got in touch to express their sorrow and offered to stay in touch just as much, or as little, as I wanted them to. My own family were loyal, steadfast and rocklike in their support and companionship – from which I drew so much strength. This post-bereavement circle with its undulating, expanded edges was a place filled with kindness, I found.

In fact, that is not quite true. Whilst family were wonderful, church people were generous and friends were understanding, there was one person who stood within that circle who was often none of those things. He was me. He was not me all the time, but occasionally he would manifest himself as one of the terrible triplets.

Mr Shouty was a version of me who was deeply intolerant of the time it was taking to heal. When I fell asleep every time I sat down, or shied away from the simplest social engagement, or melted at the thought of returning to work, he would stamp his feet and berate me for being pathetic. In my mind he looks just like me, except with a cross, red face and a permanently furrowed brow. He also has enormous clown feet. These he would stamp hard enough to make ornaments rattle on the shelves if he were dissatisfied with my behaviour. He did it once when I was walking along on a gorgeous spring morning. The sun was breaking through the clouds and turning the water in the canal into liquid gold. The birds were singing and the dog was trotting happily beside me. Caught up in the moment, I started to whistle – and immediately felt the stamping foot of

Mr Shouty come down with an almighty thud. Joy was replaced with anger, lightness with darkness and the moment was lost.

A close cousin of Mr Shouty was *Mr Angry*. He was not equipped with the clown feet of Mr Shouty. In fact, to look at him, he looked just like me, but on a bad day. Closer inspection, though, would reveal a ruddy complexion and occasional jets of steam emanating from the ears. To me, Mr Angry was a stranger, as there had rarely been a place for him in my life before. Occasionally, though, he would emerge after several months of bereavement. He never seemed bothered by the loss of Fiona, nor the sadness. Instead, he would come out at things totally unrelated. The loss of a small object or the forgetting of a shopping list would bring him charging out like a racehorse released from the gate. Sometimes, long after the 'offending incident' had gone, it would take many hours to round him up and contain him once again.

Mr Selfish was altogether different. He never made much noise, he never moved quickly, and he wrung his rather outsize versions of my hands together like Uriah Heep. As somebody with a need approached, especially an emotional one, the rate of the hand-wringing would increase. 'Keep away from me,' he would mutter. 'Don't you know I'm bereaved?' He would do it with practical needs too, exclaiming that they could not possibly be met by a *widower*. On his worst days he would moan about the person with the audacity to step out and use a zebra crossing in front of the car, or the invisible computer which had changed a traffic light from amber to red. Mr Selfish was hard-going, especially on the days when the physical and emotional needs of others could not actually be met. Nobody likes a know-it-all.

There is no normal

The thing which has surprised me in all that I have written about here, is that I would have predicted none of it. I would have expected *other* people to be upset in the shops, or put off their food, or standing at the grave, or crying over the calendar. These are not the kind of things to be done by any version of Richard Littledale which I recognize. The thing is, Richard Littledale has never been in this situation before – so how is anybody to predict how he will react?

Years ago, when I was studying the grieving process as a trainee pastor, I learned to identify it as a linear process through which the bereaved person must pass. The stages are horrible and challenging and unwelcome – but at least there is some kind of order to them. Each stage feeds into the next, which informs the next and so the journey progresses until light is glimpsed through the end of the tunnel. Sadly, it is not nearly as neat as that. Grief does not progress in a neat linear fashion. If it were an artwork it would be full of Jackson Pollock's spatters rather than Mondrian's straight lines. None of us get to choose how our grieving is done, nor how we progress through it. We do not get to write the script of this particular play – only to act our way through it. Maybe the only right way to do grieving is your way.

7

What to Pack

Many years ago, when I was a Cub Scout, we used to play a game called 'when I went to camp'. Sitting in a circle, each player would say the words, 'When I went to camp, I packed into my rucksack a . . .' Subsequent players would then repeat that phrase, followed by a list of all the objects of all the previous participants. In the end, the whole thing would become impossible to remember. I have no desire to burden any reader with such a list. However, I thought that before closing this book, I would like to suggest some items to pack for your journey through the land of grief. The idea was born when a friend wrote to me just recently to tell me that her husband was dying. Not wanting to simply say I was 'sorry', nor to burden her with a weighty and unwelcome list of advice, I picked out just two things to say – namely that time together is precious and that conversations with each other are to be treasured like gold. It is in a similar spirit that I write this list to conclude the book. It is not exhaustive, and it is undoubtedly biased by my own particular experience – but hopefully it is helpful.

When you travel through the land of grief, make sure that you take with you:

A photo of the one you have lost

You won't always need to look at it. Some days you will forget it is there, and other days looking at it will make the tears flow so much you will wish you had never brought it along. Far worse than that, though, would be to wish you had it and find that it was not there.

A pocketful of promises

I say a 'pocketful' because you will need different ones for different days. Sometimes you need the big promises which cover today, tomorrow and always – such as 'And surely I am with you always, to the very end of the age' (Matt. 28:20). Other times you need the smaller, more intimate promises, like 'do not be afraid' (available on 365 different occasions in the Bible). You need enough to pick and choose but not so many as to overwhelm you. As good as they are for you, some days you will find it hard to swallow them – especially the big ones.

The scent of heaven

Most of us have some place which we regard as heaven on earth, or at least a hint of heaven on earth. About fourteen months before she died, Fiona insisted on climbing to the very top of the Sugarloaf Mountain in the Brecon Beacons. It was really too much for her, but she was insistent on reaching the top. Half way up, we stopped, both panting a little, and gazed down at the patchwork view spread out below. 'Fix it in your mind,' she said. 'Then you can come back to it whenever you need it.' How right she was, and how often I have. All of us who are alive have not seen heaven yet – so we must use our senses to help us picture it.

The right phone numbers

Note that I did not say to bring your entire phone book. Amongst the many people who have doubtless said to you to 'ring any time' there are two or three where you know that they really mean it. The conversation need not be long, or especially coherent – but you need to be in a position to have it, so make sure you've got their number.

A notebook and pen

. . . after all, you might want to write a postcard or two!

8

Books for Company

Resources for the Traveller in the Land of Grief

I rarely travel anywhere without something to read on the way. You may find that any or all of these are good companions in the land of grief. They have all been of enormous help to me.

David Baldacci, *One Summer* (London: Macmillan, 2011).

Dietrich Bonhoeffer, *The Cost of Discipleship* (London: SCM, 1959).

Dietrich Bonhoeffer, *Letters and Papers from Prison* (London: Fontana, 1959).

Martin Buber, *I and Thou* (New York: Touchstone, 1971).

Sheila Cassidy, *Sharing the Darkness* (London: Darton, Longman & Todd, 1988).

Jane Eisenhauer, *Travellers' Tales: Poetry from Hospice* (London: HarperCollins, 1989).

Paul Fiddes, *The Creative Suffering of God* (Oxford: Clarendon Press, 1988).

Stanley Hauerwas, *Suffering Presence* (Notre Dame, IN: Notre Dame Press, 1986).

E.N. Jackson, *The Many Faces of Grief* (London: SCM, 1978).

Kirk Byron Jones, *The Jazz of Preaching* (Nashville, TN: Abingdon Press, 2004).

Richard Littledale, *Journey: The Way of the Disciple* (Milton Keynes: Authentic, 2017).

Malcolm Muggeridge, *Something Beautiful for God* (London: HarperCollins, 1972).

Gordon Mursell, *Out of the Deep: Prayer as Protest* (London: Darton, Longman & Todd, 1989).

Henri Nouwen, *The Wounded Healer* (New York: Doubleday, 1990).

Robert Twycross, ed., *Mud and Stars: The Impact of Hospice Experience on the Church's Ministry of Healing* (Oxford: Sobell, 1991).

Sheldon Vanauken, *A Severe Mercy* (London: Hodder & Stoughton, 2011).

9

Bothies on the Way

Recently I heard an enthusiastic walker talking about bothies. Bothies are shelters in remote places, accessible only on foot or mountain bike. Most were formerly cottages occupied by itinerant seasonal workers, and now offer little more than four walls, a roof and a fireplace. They are not permanent homes, nor even holiday homes. Rather, they are shelters along the way – a place for the weary traveller to shelter from the elements and gather their strength before moving on again. It is in such a way that I offer the resources below to you. They may provide some shelter along the way . . .

Sue Ryder Online Community

Sue Ryder is an organization known for its palliative and neurological care. However, when they opened their online community in 2016, a curious thing happened. They discovered that the vast majority of those accessing the community (now approximately 17,000 every month) were not those undergoing end of life care, but the bereaved. The online community is a safe, kind, moderated online space to share your experiences of grief, and to find out whether others are experiencing the same things. They nearly always are. You can access the community here: https://support.sueryder.org/community

Cruse Bereavement Care

Cruse was founded in 1959 by a group of widows caring for each other. They took their name from the story of Elijah and the widow of Zarephath in 1 Kings 17. So long as she cared for him, her 'cruse' of oil did not run dry. Cruse is all about supporting people through the experience of bereavement, no matter how long it may take. They offer counselling, resources and very often the opportunity for those who have been through bereavement to care for others in the same situation. You can access your local Cruse group here: https://www.cruse.org.uk/get-help/local-services

Sands Stillbirth & Neonatal Death Charity

Sands provide dedicated support and information for parents who are grieving the loss of a child through stillbirth or neonatal death. As well as printed resources and an online community, they offer a bereavement support app. You can find out more about them here: https://www.sands.org.uk/

Maggie's

Built in the grounds of NHS cancer hospitals, Maggie's offer practical, emotional and social support to those living with cancer and their families. If you have lost a loved one to cancer, you will find that they can either offer bereavement support or direct you to it. You can find your nearest Maggie's centre here: https://www.maggiescentres.org/our-centres/

There are, of course, many others. However, these may provide a starting point.

Postcards with Pictures

These 'Postcards from the Land of Grief 'were originally published on my blog. You can find them at http://bit.ly/postcardsfromgrief along with the pictures which accompanied them. Each postcard has a comments box where you can interact with me, or with other readers. Why not drop in and take a look?

Acknowledgements

With thanks to Philip Billson and Andrew Earis, for giving 'Postcards' their voice on BBC Radio 4.

With thanks to the team at Authentic Media, for working tirelessly to place this book in your hands.

Notes

1 The Chapter I Wanted to Write

[1] Kirk Byron Jones, *The Jazz of Preaching* © Copyright 2004 by Abingdon Press. All rights reserved. Used by permission.

Postcard 13

[1] THE MAGICIAN'S NEPHEW by C.S. Lewis copyright © C.S. Lewis Pte. Ltd. 1955.

Postcard 21

[1] See 1 Corinthians 13:7,8.

4 Battered, Bruised or Shaped?

[1] Milton Keynes: Authentic, 2017.

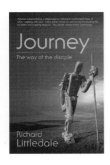

Journey
The way of the disciple

Richard Littledale

'I want people to consider their life's journey, wherever their feet might take them, as a pilgrim's way – complete with leaving home, provisions, communications, distractions and a journey's end.'

In this delightful book, Richard Littledale helps us relate the concerns of the pilgrim's life to our own, and how this practice can help us walk a God-guided path. Enriched by the writings and artwork of other pilgrims, you'll be drawn along the trail, meet fellow travellers, have time for reflection, and find yourself changed by the journey.

978-1-84227-985-4

Authentic

We trust you enjoyed reading this book from Authentic. If you want to be informed of any new titles from this author and other releases you can sign up to the Authentic newsletter by scanning below:

Online:
authenticmedia.co.uk

Follow us: